Wrong Turn on the Information Superhighway

Education and the Commercialization of the Internet

Wrong Turn on the Information Superhighway

Education and the Commercialization of the Internet

BETTINA FABOS

Foreword by Carmen Luke

Teachers College, Columbia University
New York and London

Published by Teachers College Press, 1234 Amsterdam Avenue, New York, NY 10027

Library of Congress Cataloging-in-Publication Data

Fabos, Bettina.
    Wrong turn on the information superhighway : education and the commercialization of the Internet / Bettina Fabos.
    p. cm.
    Includes bibliographical references and index.
    ISBN 0-8077-4475-1 (cloth : alk. paper) — ISBN 0-8077-4474-3 (pbk. : alk. paper)
    1. Internet in education. 2. Internet advertising. 3. Commercialism in schools. I. Title.
    LB1044.87.F33   2004
371.33'467'8—dc22   2003068749

ISBN 0-8077-4474-3 (paper)
ISBN 0-8077-4475-1 (cloth)

Printed on acid-free paper
Manufactured in the United States of America

11   10   09   08   07   06   05   04   8   7   6   5   4   3   2   1

To Christopher, Olivia, and Sabine,
my partners in life

"Whatever is honored in a culture will be cultivated there."

—Plato

Contents

PART II:
A COMMERCIAL HIGHWAY IN EVERY CLASSROOM

Foreword

When the Brazilian government recently moved to abandon costly Microsoft agreements and adopt free, open source software as its operating standard, a disgruntled Microsoft official commented, without any apparent irony, that his firm advocated the right of "free choice." Yes—the free choice to have the country's information infrastructure dominated by a single commercial firm. Brazil's decision to go with software from the public domain reminds us that there are alternative visions to a fully commercialized information superhighway.

During the heady days of the "digital revolution" and advent of the "information superhighway," could any of us—educators, bureaucrats, or otherwise—have imagined the future of the worldwide web and digital technologies as one co-opted by capital and the market? I think not. Throughout the 1990s, a powerful discourse on advertising, social, and academic commentary began to explicate developments and promises of "cyberspace." Government and industry promises of universal access to a global library of knowledge were met with arguments that cautioned against the hype, optimism, and opportunism and those that celebrated the democratic potential of global information access, of new social and intercultural relations, of diverse virtual communities, and of a truly emancipatory educational tool.

Yet, in the history of 20th-century media of communication, "moving" pictures, radio, and TV all heralded great educational potential but all quickly succumbed to commercialism and the logic of capital markets. Regardless of their cultural and social effects and consequences, these three "big media" of the last century became powerful modes for teaching consumerist values and behaviors, combining to make the largest global forum for public pedagogies of mass culture—itself largely steeped in the American dream factory of popular culture: image, identity, lifestyle. Whatever's on the screen, microwaves, or airwaves is purchasable—a buy button or shopping cart is never far away.

Bettina Fabos brings a communications background to this timely topic of internet use in schools Her instinct here is to situate educational issues in a larger economic, socio-cultural, and historical communications context, to show that no knowledge or communications medium is outside ideological, political, and economic interests. This is still an important lesson for educators, particularly as developments like the Bush Administration's recent *No Child Left Behind* initiative have the effect of re-instilling an ideology that media and modes of learning—whether reading series, textbooks, or new media—can be objective, scientific, and neutral. As research in the 1980s pointed out, educational print media have long been dominated by corporate interests and ideological subtexts (Apple & Christian-Smith, 1991).

This situation, of course, extends to the political economy of mass communications media, well documented in neomarxian communications studies (e.g., Schiller, 1989). It is in this tradition that Fabos depicts the commercialization of the internet, its incursion into everyday life, and its educational implications—not as a Luddite but rather as a means to push past the acritical "enthusiasm" that seems to dominate educational debates over media. As she argues, "the political economy perspective offers a platform from which to ask important questions about information access, content control, and the future of the internet as an educational and democratic information tool."

Advertisers have always pushed the educational potential of high speed computing, connectivity, and the web—families can learn together, play together, and anyone anywhere can communicate with others or access information at the click of a mouse. Learning, entertainment, and (home-based) business were all rolled into one screen-based experience. Parental moral panics about kids' attitudes and wayward tendencies could always be resolved by promises of home-learning centers and happy families logging-in together, learning together. A host of "net nanny" software promised children's protection and parental control and surveillance. But something happened along the way from early innocent and idealist visions of the global community, the global classroom, and the connected learning community. Not only was it kids that taught parents how to navigate the web, use e-cash, set up software and browser preferences, and so forth, but advertisers quickly picked up that kids didn't mind advertising since their entire life experience was based in commercial and multimedia culture—from MTV to console gaming and the massive range of cross-media-marketed e-toys. Online commercial pitches to kids and teens—who are in fact the frontline at the screen—bypass parental concerns over commercialization altogether. Teachers and librarians too often just sit in witness of students' preferences for, and trust in, commercial search engines over more sober and less glitzy portals, and for the brash marketing, indeed narrow-casting, techniques of commercial search engines that lure users down specific and narrow information pathways.

The internet is the new frontier of mass culture. It has become the new library, ticket office, shopping mall, auction house, doctor's office, classroom, and office. Along the way, from an online stop to shop, then pay bills, next a click to get the weekend weather, and over to the latest sports scores, we now encounter the old 1950s billboard clutter—"side of the road" gateways peppered with ad site banners, pop-ups and pop-unders, commercial portals with seductive sponsored links, often to "mousetrapped" sites that lock us in much like stores lure us into the "sale" trap through promotional enticements. If anything, the web today mirrors, if not exceeds, our mall-cruising experience—its sophisticated visual and multimedia menu provides a lavish consumer fest where knowledge, information, consumer products, and pop culture all melt into the one common denominator of the market. And one doesn't have to dig deep to discover the profitable synergies between established corporate giants in the media, telecommunications, and computer industries who are in fact shaping the content, access, cartography, and future of the web.

Fabos draws out these issues in ways that should not only alert us to the traps and risks of commercial e-culture and of educational hype, but in ways that highlight the value a cultural studies and communications approach can offer mainstream education. This interdisciplinary lens frames the questions she asks of educators and students in her year-long case study of three midwestern schools. Her concern isn't with teacher and student "IT literacy," competence in web search techniques, or webpage-evaluation skills. Rather, she asks *why* most of the teachers in her study were not alarmed by encroaching privatization and commercialization of the web.

Arguably, the commercialization of net culture was inevitable. Yet that should not stifle scholarly debate and strategic resistance to government policies that encourage market incursions into educational content and, by association, the "new" learner-centered e-pedagogies. There *are* alternatives—EdNA or Education Network Australia

(http://www.edna.edu.au) is a good example of the possibility of a
non-commercial education portal. It is owned, managed, and funded
by Australian federal and all state government education departments reflecting government commitment and involvement—indeed,
a hands-on approach—that would not appeal to American political
sensibilities.

In the United States and elsewhere, media education has been one
longstanding, although sporadic, alternative educational approach to
the impact of mass media and consumerism on youth. However,
efforts to equip students with critical literacy skills to challenge media
messages often serve as end-of-the-unit curriculum add-ons, and the
focus of most media literacy curricula remains fixed on traditional
broadcast media, videogames, or music videos. Where media literacy
programs include a unit on the web, the focus tends not to go beyond
website evaluation of operational features and, at best, skills for verifying the truthfulness or trustworthiness of a site.

As Fabos shows us, in light of the probably irreversible commercialization of the internet and the increasing amount of classroom time
spent online, we need, now more than ever, a strong critical literacy
component structured across the curriculum and grade levels. Beyond
school, so much of everyday life has already migrated online—clearly
educators have a responsibility to teach this and subsequent genera-
tions to ask the critical questions of the one medium of communication, sociality, and information that is today and will invariably be
even more central in their lives. Students have a right to be equipped
with evolving meta-analytic skills with which to consider how they
are being positioned, how their consumer-learner identity is crafted,
what their role and choices are, how pathways to, and the form and
content of, knowledge are shaped by the commercial interests of mar-
keteer knowledge brokers.

In *Wrong Turn on the Information Superhighway*, then, Bettina Fabos
offers much more than a critique of capital's colonization of the internet and brash incursions into education. It is, importantly, a call to
recuperate some ground in the "culture war" between those who still
believe in the liberal democratic principle of education as a public
good, and those corporate and government interests that want to
unleash the vagaries of capital and free-market principles on education. So, where do we want to go today—and tomorrow? Where
there's no commercial clutter, no forced off-ramps or mousetraps

dragging us off to some dead-end information abyss where the only bright lights are a shopping cart and buy button.

We might want to build an information environment and, indeed, economy, where there is a focal place for teaching and learning critical educational practices—for students and teachers to dialogue about how these media work, who owns them, whose interests they serve, what they and their texts try to do to us, our communities and our lives, their potential for building minds and communities, and for control and deception. As citizens and educators we may, ultimately, not be able to alter the patterns of ownership—the collaborative relationships between corporate media business, government, and globalization in ways that we would like. But we can indeed continue to work to stake out curriculum and pedagogy as sites where audiences, web-surfers, viewers, and others explore how these systems work: their ideological auspices and cultural consequences. To do so, we need more analyses of the depth and critical eye that Bettina Fabos offers us here.

Carmen Luke
January 2004

REFERENCES

Apple, M., & Christian-Smith, L. (Eds.). (1991). *The politics of the textbook*. New York: Routledge.

Schiller, H. (1989). *Culture, INC.: The corporate takeover of public expression*. New York: Oxford University Press.

Acknowledgments

I owe a great debt of thanks to many people: those who helped shape this book, but also those who helped shape its author.

Thank you, Jimmie Reeves, for telling me, way back when, that I should become a scholar. Thank you, Robert McChesney, for saying (when I was a novice doctoral student) that my research would be a valuable contribution to both communication and education. I will always have deep admiration for your work. Thank you, Richard Campbell, for inviting me to annually update and revise your masterful textbook, *Media and Culture*, easily the best critical survey of mass communication out there, and an important testament to the need for democratic media.

Thank you, Cynthia Lewis, my pillar of strength, for encouraging my ideas from the very beginning; your knowledge and advice significantly moved this research forward. Thank you, Jim Marshall, for asking the big picture questions and helping me understand the relevance of this work to a broader public—your excitement and support will be always valued. Thank you, Judy Polumbaum, for offering me grounded wisdom and many insights into internet use from a cultural studies and journalistic perspective. Thank you, John Durham Peters, for your quiet precision, and for anchoring the theoretical and historical areas of this work. Thank you, Carolyn Colvin, for being the kindest devil's advocate imaginable, always asking me to consider the other side. And thank you, David O'Shields, for reading final versions of this manuscript not once, but twice. I am indebted to your thoughtful suggestions and unwavering enthusiasm for this topic.

Thank you, University of Iowa and the Spencer Foundation, for the funding that made the research behind this book possible. Thank you, teachers, media specialists, principals, and students, who agreed to participate in this project. Thank you, Catherine Chandler, Carole Saltz, and Karl Nyberg, my editors at Teachers College Press who have deftly brought this book to publication.

Thank you, Julius Gy. Fabos and Edith Fabos (my wonderful parents), for helping me think against the common grain, for broadening my horizons in so many areas, and for putting travel above material things.

Thank you, Olivia and Sabine, my two incredible daughters, who were born over the course of researching and writing this book. You are my biggest joys, and will always be associated with this work.

And most importantly, thank you, Christopher Martin, my mentor, colleague, best friend, and husband. Thank you for being so darn smart . . . for making this book ring true, for providing constant energy and focus, for catching a fair number of misplaced modifiers, and for engaging me, constantly, in engrossing conversations about the media, education, and democracy. This book is because of you.

Introduction

When I began this book, all the students, media specialists, and teachers I talked to had great respect for the worldwide web as an educational medium. Perhaps the most passionate advocate of all was one English teacher, Steve LeRouge. Great in the classroom and passionate about the web, he was more familiar with online resources than most people. He had his students use the web for numerous class projects and even taught a special unit in webpage critique. In fact, he was so optimistic about the web in education that he made me feel as if online commercialism—the focus of my study—was no big deal. "Teachers don't have to be that savvy," he told me. "Kids know a spiel when they see one. They've been exposed to spiels all their lives. Kids do know about commercialism and they don't get taken in easily." Steve was far more worried about government efforts to filter "adult" web content from school sites than he was about internet commercialization.

But 3 years later my research was done, and I emailed some of my conclusions to Steve. As usual, he was smart and funny, but he also had a different mindset from the pure optimism he showed before. Steve was clearly getting fed up with the onslaught of commercial messages that were obstructing his students' research and learning. Indeed, his reply to me amounted to a scathing indictment of what the web had become:

> The pop-up ads alone are annoying, but many (probably most) sites also sandwich whatever article is of interest between columns of advertisements. Even pretty reputable sites like Time.com or ScientificAmerican.com throw pop-ups and columns of ads at the students; even .org sites like pbs.org want to sell you stuff at their "Shop PBS" link! For the most part, if the research topic is a traditional social issue topic like date rape or alternative fuels or sports injuries, the students can pretty much ignore the ads. But, when the research topic is a little more "edgy," the ads follow suit, and then I know I have trouble:

"Hey, Chris, c'mon over here and check out this cool bong!"
"No way, man, that's just not possible!"
"Fer real! They're usin' .50 caliber casings for the bowl!"
"Aw, that's just too whack!"

You get the idea. Do anything on designer drugs or music censorship or legalization of drugs or street racing and I spend 90 percent of my time puttin' out fires. I even had a "good" student (who, I know, wouldn't intentionally stray) get locked into a porn loop when he followed a link on F1 racing. Go figure. I had a student do a paper on disc golf this last semester. Since there are no traditional sources on the topic, his paper was almost entirely based on Internet sources. Do you have any idea how many ads there are for sports equipment and diet supplements on sports-related sites? Once he was past the blizzard of pop-ups and flashing ads, he still had to navigate the homepages, which are designed to give you no real information, but only links, which trigger another wave of pop-ups and ads. Sometimes the actual articles are three or four layers deep. Oy Vey!

Steve was now grappling with online commercialism, which has grown from annoying online ads to something much larger. And that's what this book is about. It's about what capitalism has done to the web, turning what was promised as an "information highway" into a commercial highway in every classroom. Not only has advertising become more pervasive, but commercial interests have also undermined the integrity of search engines and compromised the educational value of most of the web's vast holdings. This book is the story of how this happened, but it also concerns the steps that educators, policy makers, and citizens need to reclaim the internet for education.

The year 1995 was a pivotal one in the history of communication technology. It was the year the internet took off in schools—the most exciting communication technology in education since television, 30 years earlier. Educators, librarians, parents, and internet promoters called the new medium a library of information at children's fingertips, and identified the internet as a panacea for education. It was the year President Clinton first "challenged" all American classrooms to get onto the information superhighway, citing research that the internet would drastically help at-risk students. It was the year community members across the United States gave up their weekends to roll up their sleeves, pull cables, and wire schools. These "netdays" were heavily publicized in local papers and on local TV. Even President Clinton and Vice President Gore (who had coined the term *information superhighway*) donned their work clothes to participate in several NetDay wiring efforts.

The year 1995 was also when several high-profile advertising campaigns began promoting the internet as a key to greater knowledge and as a technology for both an educational and democratic revolution. The blitz of print and television advertisements portrayed children poised in front of their computers, enthralled with the "knowledge" pouring directly into their brains. Some ads touted that children gave up recess time to stay inside and interact online. In other ads, children magically floated above their desks, buoyed by their imagination and the online conversations they were having with real astronauts. The ads *en force* suggested that children, with their proficient keying skills and easy grasp of technology, were savvy drivers on the information highway, more adept, even, than adults.

The year 1995 was also the year that Microsoft leader Bill Gates published his bestseller *The Road Ahead*, which introduced his vision of the "Connected Learning Community" via the internet. Gates publicized the book with speeches all over the United States, expounding on the educational promise of internet technology and donating the proceeds of his book to support technology in public schools. It was the year when the internet was surely positioned as an educational technology.

Most significantly, amid the extensive campaign to exult prospects of the internet for public education, 1995 was the year that the internet became privatized. Built over the previous 3 decades with government-supported, publicly funded programs, the internet's U.S. backbone was quietly sold to telecommunications and computer giants in 1995. Thus, at the same time that the prominent rhetoric about education and knowledge was in ascendance, powerful corporate interests were reshaping the internet as a commercial tool. And its ubiquity was growing. By 2000, more than 97% of U.S. schools had internet access; a majority of U.S. homes and offices were connected as well. In 5 short years, the internet had become a mass medium, achieving this benchmark more quickly than any communication technology before (Kurtz, 2000).

To any student of media history, the commercialization of the internet should come as no surprise. Every major communication technology, despite its initial promise as a medium for greater education and democracy, has been overtaken by commercial interests. Film, which promoters claimed would replace textbooks and make all learning visual, did not last long as an educational technology: Its high cost of production resulted in dreadful educational film content. The slickest educational film productions were often just thinly veiled corporate public relations pieces for the classroom. Film would serve the entertainment industry, not education.

Radio, which was more affordable and accessible than film, had greater promise as an educational medium. Initially developed, like the internet, by grassroots efforts and government investment, radio found teachers and students as its earliest adopters. Radio's early success in education, however, was soon squashed by the intense power and lobbying efforts of the commercial radio industry. U.S. public airwaves were won by commercial interests in 1934, although unlike with the internet, there was intense debate over the matter. Then came television, which was hobbled as an educational tool because it was based on radio's commercial model from its inception. Furthermore, the high cost of broadcast TV production made it an uneconomical educational tool. All these technologies would not serve education, no matter how promising. The internet, it now seems, is following suit.

Today, the information highway looks more like a shopping mall than a library. By 1999, researchers had already determined that 83% of the web served commercial purposes, with only 6% serving science/education (defined as serving university, college, and research interests) (Lawrence & Giles, 1999, p. 107). Commercial advertisements, most commonly in the forms of interactive banner, pop-up, and pop-under displays, dominate the web. But more consequentially, commercial services have successfully managed to route users from *all* that the worldwide web has to offer into an increasingly finite and incestuous web of commercial enterprise.

First, commercial web-navigation services, which initially generated income through web display ads, now make much more revenue by directing users to the websites of clients who pay for such placement. Content directories such as LookSmart and America Online (AOL) and commercial search engine providers such as Overture accept payments for prominently displaying commercial websites within their directories or search-result lists. Overture's strategies, which are now common practice in the search engine industry, illustrate the extent to which commercial online ventures are willing to sacrifice content and neutrality for profit. Even the one search engine provider that uses rigorous methods to maintain integrity in search-es—Google—still ends up with search results that are inevitably skewed by the enormity of commercial sites now dominating the web.

Then there are the intensifying efforts among the largest media companies to funnel web content (and web users) into increasingly narrow channels, which are either owned by them or are in partner-ship with them. With their dominance as internet service providers (ISPs) and email and instant messaging service providers, and with their strong brand-name identification, companies such as Time Warner, Yahoo!, and Microsoft can more easily control the way people use the web and the breadth of information people can locate online. This is not to say that there are not incredible, valuable, and wonder-ful websites that offer a host of different ideas and a wealth of infor-mation. In this book I make the argument that the internet does indeed belong in the classroom. No technology since radio has so captivated educators' attention. The medium has enormous potential as a place to share ideas, as a place to publish school projects, and as a place for educators to join together and exchange teaching methods and lesson plans. It has enormous potential as a research tool, as a library, and as a laboratory. As a vehicle for written, audio, and visual communica-tion, the internet has unprecedented flexibility and adaptability.

Indeed, citizens and schools already use the internet for education and many are using it well. But the end result of the internet's now extensive commercialization is that users continue to be directed to an abundance of commercial sites—some valuable, many not—while other potentially valuable online materials are being marginalized as public and nonprofit online spaces are becoming increasingly difficult to find. This is both a problem for educators, who have no organized response to these developments, and all citizens, for the success of the internet as a democratic medium and educational tool is dependent upon a plurality of voices.

A GUIDE TO THIS BOOK

This book investigates the implications that the privatized, commer-cialized internet has as an educational resource for students, particu-larly those in grades K–12. My perspective is informed by studies of *political economy*, which try to understand social practices by analyzing the political and economic connections between macro-level power structures (e.g., capitalist enterprise, private ownership of the means of production) and the development of social systems (e.g., schools, the internet). The approach is based on the presumption that the political and economic context of a social system dramatically influences the system's makeup. When one is considering the internet as a private enterprise, the political economy perspective offers a platform from which to ask important questions about information access, content control, and the future of the internet as an educational and democratic information tool. This perspective enables me to investigate to what degree the internet can and will be an information highway, as its early promoters called it, or the opposite: a commercial highway filled with advertisements, "buy" buttons, and "information" placed by undisclosed corporate sponsors.

I use two methodological approaches to examine potential inroads of commercialism into the classroom: historical analysis and case study. As such, the book falls into two distinct parts. In Part I, I historically situate present-day internet educational content in terms of previous educational media (film, radio, and television) and make comparisons between internet content and the content of earlier media, all of which became dominated by private interests. In Part II, I complement this historical analysis with an explanation of how educators approach and discuss internet content for classroom use. Besides documenting nationwide trends, I offer the results of a year-long case study that tracked the everyday use of websites in three technologically advanced midwestern U.S. schools within the same progressive school district. With this case study I investigate the degree to which commercial interests have entered present-day classroom culture via the web, and the way teachers and students understand and evaluate such web content.

I conclude the book by considering the future of the internet in schools and point to ways in which the worldwide web could be better used as an educational tool. First, I argue that we should work to better understand the internet as a commercialized mass medium and help teachers expand their critique beyond individual pages of the web to include an evaluation of the internet as a commercially compromised information superhighway. Second, I assert that we should take the next step in the project of the information superhighway. Yes, the *highway* infrastructure has been built, but there has been shamefully little attention paid to the *information* part—the actual educational content of the web.

PART I

History and Context

CHAPTER 1

Giddy Prophesies
and Commercial Ventures:
The History of Educational Media

The motion picture is destined to revolutionize our educational system and...in a few years it will supplant largely, if not entirely, the use of textbooks.

—Thomas Edison, 1922

Wedded to a deep identification with both science and religion, technology is the center of [American] civic life, the one unquestioned good, before which we both worship in awe and collapse in fear....
Our national storytelling is, to an unusual extent, embedded in the history of technology.

—James Carey, 1997

Technology has a special place in American culture. It is ineluctably wedded to the American philosophy of progress and we romanticize its capabilities. We trust that scientific achievements will make the world a better and safer place (Robins & Webster, 1999). Our faith in technology has certainly been prevalent in the social sphere of education. Since the turn of the 20th century and the development of communication technology, educational literature and the popular press have been filled with visions of technology-laden schools and giddy prophesies of how the latest medium will improve learning across the educational spectrum. As educational historians have noted, each new technology that was introduced into schools spurred an enormous amount of enthusiasm among educators, administrators, and technology advocates (e.g., Cuban, 1986). The use of Victrolas, film projectors, radios, televisions, cassette recorders, video, computers, CD-ROMs, and the internet have all been presumed to rejuvenate or reform education. Not surprisingly, the hopeful discourses for each medium throughout this "Age of Information" are so similar that predictions for one educational technology can easily be substituted for another.

Each new technology was believed to solve chronic *administrative problems* in schools. New technology would increase classroom efficiency, solve teacher shortages, and rectify "bad" teaching (e.g., Levenson & Stasheff, 1952). Administrators could also point to the important technological and communication skills, such as "earmindedness" in the case of radio, as well as speaking, writing, and production techniques that students would need for future employment (e.g., Atkinson, 1938). But most important, new technology was believed to aid the *teaching process*. Records, films, radio, television, and the internet would enhance "dull" school life and tired textbooks by bringing the real world, expert knowledge, and enriching content into the classroom (e.g., Marsh, 1936).

Technologically mediated content would motivate students to want to learn (e.g., Atkinson, 1938; Darrow, 1932). New technology was celebrated as an impetus for student-centered and collaborative learning, and teachers were encouraged to view their students as "coplanners and coworkers" who, beyond listening or watching, would become *active* and engaged participants in the classroom (e.g., Atkinson, 1938). With the aid of media technology, students—everyone—could learn beyond the classroom through quality educational and entertainment programming. The technology, in other words, would inspire endless learning opportunities. With every new medium came these claims about better learning environments, better teachers, smarter students, smarter people, a more responsible civic environment, and a better world.

TECHNOLOGY, YES, BUT WHAT ABOUT CONTENT?

Since pedagogy has always been the crux of most educational-technology rhetoric, it is not surprising that pedagogy is also the focus of existing historical research. Over the past 2 decades, historians—representing both protechnologist and antitechnologist camps—have considered the effectiveness of educational technology's impact on the teaching *process*. They have asked, for example, whether or not a particular technology stimulated student participation, changed the structure of teacher-student relations, or enabled teachers to convey information more efficiently. In their endeavor to identify a pattern or a "cycle" of technological use in the classroom from decade to decade, however, these writers have overlooked important differences between technologies by eventually encompassing a very wide span of communication advances under the singular term *technology*. Some firmly believe that the technology is always good but that unwilling teachers make it fail; others blame the ponderous nature of the technology itself and assert that it's not what teachers need to teach well. The focus is always on the machine as it helps or hurts the teaching process.

While pedagogy may indeed be a significant part of the story of classroom technology, analyzing the *content* that is carried over these new technologies is an equally important—and drastically overlooked—part of the educational-technology story. What were students listening to or watching in schools, and why? What forces controlled educational-program content, and how did this control ultimately determine the way it was used in schools? What, if any, ulterior motives existed to get a particular kind of content in the classroom? If teachers are the gatekeepers of technology who have time and again rejected educational technology, I would like to reconsider what teachers and administrators were ultimately rejecting in the march to put new technology in schools. Were they rejecting the technology per se, or were they rejecting the programming delivered via particular technologies?

FILM IN THE CLASSROOM

When considering the history of educational technology, it is necessary to make an important distinction. Some classroom technologies had been fully developed as commercial enterprises *before* they entered the educational market. Other technologies began as experiments among educators and hobbyists, and then *afterward* became more broadly defined as a commercial media.

Film technology came to education via the first path: as an industry afterthought. Celluloid film was adapted for motion pictures in the

1880s, and in only 6 short years, the potential of film as a commercial theatrical enterprise was evident. Only after 1910 did commercial companies begin to tap the education market with its new genre of "educationals" (Saettler, 1990).

Although the possibilities of moving images in the classroom was certainly inspiring for many, the most vocal film advocates represented companies with a stake in getting schools to buy film projectors. Thomas Edison, for example, who had taken part in inventing both film production and projection, was one of the most enthusiastic promoters of classroom film use. Consequently, Edison became for film very much like what Bill Gates is today for the internet: a huge advocate of his medium in schools; Edison prophesied that film would render books obsolete and would stimulate learning beyond people's imagination, changing school life within a decade (Saettler, 1990).

Between 1900 and 1920, a number of other companies formed in hopes of taking advantage of the developing school-film market. Most of them began in the film projector business and accumulated film collections in order to ensure greater equipment sales and extend the scope of their business. As far as these film collections were concerned, size was far more important than quality. In other words, the films came from just about anywhere: Hollywood (film flops repurposed for education or outtakes salvaged from the cutting-room floor and spliced to fit an educational theme); the U.S. government (dated war propaganda films and others about agriculture and health issues); corporations (public relations attempts to inform students—in a one-sided sort of way—about their corporate philosophies, histories, and product lines). The Ford Motor Company, for example, enlisted its extensive film production facilities to create the "Ford Education Library," which was devised as a far-reaching public relations effort to indirectly promote the Ford company, cars, and driving, in schools. Only a small number of educational films were actually produced by educational-film companies. These were very low budget, often consisting of a single talking head and a few essential close-ups. Like most of the Hollywood flops/outtakes, government propaganda, or corporate advertising, these films were generally undesirable for classroom use.

Since educators were not consulted as classroom films were put together, and since the resulting selections contained films of remarkably bad quality and pervasive advertising appeals, teachers didn't trust either the films or the profit motives of film-production companies (McClusky, 1937). By and large, teachers were skeptical of the increasingly powerful business community in the beginning decades of the 20th century. As they are today, schools had been a constant target of businesses ever since public education began in the early 19th century (Fones-Wolf, 1994; Molnar, 1996). But when the Depression hit, teacher distrust was magnified as local companies closed down, decreasing school income and creating social turmoil. Schools were further hurt when business organizations such as the chamber of commerce began to call for the modernization and streamlining of education practices. In the spirit of greater efficiency, business leaders proposed reducing school taxes, school budgets, and teacher salaries. Included in this rhetoric was the necessary employment of educational technology (i.e., film) to replace inefficient and costly teaching methods. Not surprisingly, educators were not receptive. Indeed, many leading educators were radically critical of American business and began to openly criticize business practices, as well as the free enterprise system (Fones-Wolf, 1994).

With such antipathy toward a corporate agenda in the classroom during the 1920s and 1930s, no wonder educators recoiled at the many infomercial (and other) films that attempted to pass for education. Interestingly, Saettler (1990) reports that colleges and universities cleared their libraries of advertising films in 1923, saying that this type of propaganda could not possibly meet educational objectives (p. 112). As such, commercial educational film ventures seemed to be doomed from the beginning. They couldn't bear the expense of producing educationally useful film content, and the alternative—cheap productions and infomercials—did not move teachers to embrace the medium.

Hopeful that carefully produced educational content had enormous potential in schools, F. Dean McClusky (1937), a school director and university instructor with expertise in visual education, offered three suggestions:

1. Companies producing educational films had to work with educators, "not theatrical producers or by any others with whom the production and distribution of motion pictures is a side line or medium for propaganda or purely a commercial enterprise."
2. These educators would be appointed by an advisory board, which would "blueprint needs, conduct research, and vali-

date materials." The board would operate in a nonprofit framework, and no board member would be able to financially benefit from their position as advisory board member.

3. The commercial producers would only be able to market educational films and ancillary materials that were approved by the advisory board; a service motive would have to come before a profit motive; and the company could in no way bend to special interests (p. 26).

Such collaborations never happened, because film was too expensive and difficult a medium for commercial film education companies (and educators working alone) to produce educationally relevant films. The economics of the medium, in other words, influenced the educational content, and the educational content failed. As such, film lost its luster in the classroom; indeed, it never really had a chance as a primary educational tool.

RADIO IN THE CLASSROOM

The story of educational radio is also one plagued by issues of quality content and educator control over the medium. The first educational radio programs were broadcast to schools in the early 1920s, just as teachers were losing faith in educational films and their content. As a new school technology, however, radio was a considerably different medium from film and, as I will argue, had considerably more potential in being widely embraced and used in schools.

Radio differed from film on three levels. First, when school broadcasts began there wasn't much inkling of radio's commercial potential. It was understood broadly as a medium controlled and inspired by individual inventiveness, and for the greater public good. Widely celebrated and initially used as an education tool during its first 5 years as a mass medium, radio did not fully develop as a commercial enterprise *before* it was used in schools, as film had been. Second, despite the huge significance of the invention, radio was a rather uncomplicated technology to master and utilize. If young adults could buy radio transmitters and receiver kits and obtain access to the airwaves (as they had been doing in radio's early years), so could educators. Perhaps more significant, radio production didn't require special cameras, costly film stock, shooting, film labs and film development, editing skills, and distribution centers. Consequently, it wasn't out of the realm of possibility for educators to produce radio programs and thus control their own educational content. Third, as a medium with unprecedented reach, one radio broadcast could target more listeners than could any medium before it. As I will discuss, this was a plus for educational radio, but also would lead to its demise.

Like the early internet, early radio was a crude but tremendously thrilling communication tool used by hobbyists and students in engineering schools. The first radio broadcasters, like the first internet users, were hacker types who saw the incredible democratic potential of the medium: Private citizens could communicate across vast distances without relying upon either the government or a corporation. Mostly middle- and upper-class boys with time to tinker, these radio hobbyists relished the novelty of speaking to complete strangers in the "ether." Instructions for assembling a homemade radio—in magazines, wireless manuals, children's books, and Boy Scout guides—spurred airwave exploration (Douglas, 1987). High schools were an important petri dish for early radio as they encouraged clubs to promote radio even further. Young boys joined radio clubs, held club meetings over the public airwaves, staged competitions between clubs, and engaged in what became a highly collaborative and addictive activity. When young radio operators communicated with rescue crews during the 1912 Titanic disaster (helping to save hundreds of lives), radio developed a heroic luster, spurring even more hobbyists to join the wireless scene. But the ship-to-shore communication effort also signaled radio's strategic significance to military operations. Hobbyists were ordered off the air during World War I; it wasn't until 1920 that the public airwaves were open again for exploration.

This time, a new crop of radio hobbyists emerged across the United States and Canada. They played music and news to listening friends a few nights a week and ushered in a new era of broadcast (rather than point-to-point) radio. Educators at universities began establishing their own educational stations, and advertising-supported commercial ventures began to spring up (Douglas, 1987; Kellner, 1990; Smulyan, 1994). The popular press celebrated radio's entertainment, educational, political, and religious potential and called the technology "an autonomous force, capable of revolutionizing American culture" (Douglas, 1987, p. xv). Every radio listener could have the best seat in the auditorium, in effect attending a super radio university that would educate the world (leveling class distinctions and erasing Ivy-league elitism), create greater political awareness, and enable access to religious sermons. Radio was of special significance to the poor, the elderly, the infirm, and people in rural communities, who couldn't fully participate in American democracy. Indeed, these press accounts heralded radio as a means for ending isolation, bringing the world together, fostering an educated and democratic citizenry, and providing unending social enrichment.

The Potential of Educational Radio

In part because educators controlled a good number of the first radio stations, the popular rhetoric about radio's potential in education dominated early perceptions of the medium. Reminiscent of claims during the early 1990s that the internet was an "information superhighway" or a "universe of knowledge" (Clinton, 1997b), radio was framed as a "transmitter of information" (Zook, 1936) and a "university of the air" (Ickes, 1936). Indeed, with their own experimental stations, educators were quite busy trying to realize radio's educational potential. Between 1922 and 1926, experimental radio lessons were broadcast from commercial, university-based, or nonprofit stations within local and regional areas. Similar to the internet "NetDay" installation efforts during the 1990s, state departments of education organized programs to encourage radio installation (Atkinson, 1938), and smaller schools, with the help of local volunteers, wired their own buildings. Some schools bought radio receivers outright, and other schools listened on borrowed or donated sets.

Because educational radio programs could be broadcast into homes and businesses as well as into schools, broadcast radio became a means for extending learning to people in far-off venues and a valuable public relations tool for promoting awareness and excitement about education by radio. Homemakers listening at home often became the most adamant supporters of a school's investment in radio technology. Schools also began to use radio to communicate educational matters on a daily basis, hold PTA meetings and teachers forums, and enlighten taxpayers about the need for high-quality education. The majority of school broadcasts related to the curriculum, however. Early broadcasts included music appreciation courses, political addresses, public speeches and debates, radio lectures delivered by local or regional teachers/experts or played on phonographs, and live dramalogues or storytelling. Some schools with shortwave receivers could receive international broadcasts.

By 1929, radio education became more organized as educators banded together to establish nonprofit "schools of the air." Many of these schools operated in the Midwest, especially in Wisconsin, Iowa, and Ohio. One of the first of these was the Ohio School of the Air, which operated between 1929 and 1937 under the direction of Ben Darrow, an indefatigable advocate of educational radio. This radio education effort, which had a listener base that extended to Canada, began, like the others, with generous state support: $40,000 was appropriated in 1928 for its first 2 years of operation. When the Depression caused a school-funding crisis during the early 1930s, the Ohio School of the Air was able to survive because of continued state appropriations.

The considerable amount of funding given to educational radio covered the schools' technical, administrative, and material costs, not the cost of providing content. The content for the Ohio School of the Air was provided by enthusiastic—and largely unpaid—teachers and local experts, who collaborated for the love and excitement of bringing education to radio. A huge amount of time and effort was involved in planning the curriculum, finding and rehearsing decent talent, promoting the programs, and distributing lesson leaflets to schools. The programs fell into a daily schedule between 2 and 2:40 p.m. Beginning with an announcer asking students to rise and sing to an organ performance of "America the Beautiful," the program continued with three units, with one directed to upper grades (e.g., current events, French or chemistry, literature, Constitution and citizenship, and drama), another to intermediate grades (e.g., nature study, literature, and health), and a third to the lower grades (e.g., story plays and rhythmics, geography, and music). Music was played between subject units so schools with receivers in larger rooms or auditoriums (and not individual classrooms) could adequately get one group of students out and another one in.

Although these radio programs necessarily generated limited student interaction during the broadcasts—a perpetual drawback of radio education—teachers were encouraged to raise questions before and after a broadcast, invite comments and correspondence, and engage their students in critical-thinking activities. With palpable and growing excitement among educators about the future of radio education, 176 broadcast licenses were issued to colleges and universities alone between 1921 and 1925 (McChesney, 1994). Perhaps much of this excitement had to do with the novelty of the medium, the positive buzz in the press, and the sometimes excellent listening opportunities available to students. Perhaps another reason could have been that this medium, for the time being, was controlled in large part by educators and was an honest and earnest civic effort with the best interests of students and the public good in mind. But radio "failed" in schools. Why? Because commercial radio overwhelmed educational-radio initiatives. The technology itself was educationally useful, but commercial imperatives sidelined educational-radio content, and subsequently educational radio disappeared.

The Growth of Commercialized Educational Radio

As publicly funded schools of the air and local nonprofit content providers continued to develop educational-radio content and inspire more radio use in schools throughout the 1920s, there was a simultaneous development: Commercialized radio also was becoming even more available, gradually pushing out nonprofit ventures and celebrating the numerous informational, educational, and entertainment opportunities it would bring. Some radio historians have noted that the financial costs of sustaining a nonprofit station was the reason so many educational stations went under (Frost, 1937). Others have pointed to the commercial radio stations' forcing out the "competition" (Atkinson, 1938; Hill, 1942). Saettler (1990) offers another compelling reason, arguing that the U.S. government, which had the authority to license stations, endorsed a "philosophy of commercial radio" and applied the same commercial standards to nonprofit radio as it set for commercial stations. These high production standards were so costly to abide by that they forced educational stations to withdraw their operations (p. 204). In any case, the number of educational stations had decreased at an alarming rate by the late 1920s.

Commercial radio stations quickly outnumbered nonprofit stations and also began to dominate educational radio. Local and regional commercial stations had already welcomed the free educational content supplied by educators, which could fill time slots not yet taken by sponsored programming. Soon, however, networks began producing ad-supported educational programs themselves. It was shows like NBC's *Walter Damrosch Music Appreciation Hour* (circa 1928) that put a stamp of approval on the radio industry's inroads in education. Damrosch had a 50-piece orchestra at his disposal and discussed orchestral music with such energy, charm, and expertise that schools without radios invested in new receivers just to hear the national broadcast (NBC was the most powerful network at the time). Other schools of the air avoided programming on Friday afternoons, knowing that the *Damrosch Hour* would have the largest draw. The radio industry hyped the educational potential of these sorts of programs and presented them as examples of noble public service rather than profit-seeking ventures (McChesney, 1994). NBC, for example, pledged to "only sell that amount of advertising necessary to subsidize first-rate noncommercial programming" (p. 16). A number of high-profile educators even worked with NBC and other commercial networks or stations to produce such "high-quality" (albeit ad-supported) content. Many educators even began to feel that ads were a necessary means of increasing the quality of an educational broadcast.

As more nonprofit educational radio stations went under, NBC invested in even more educational programming and organized the Standard School Broadcast as "an important National Broadcasting Company feature" beginning in the 1928–29 school year. Likewise, CBS (which established its network in 1927) began the American School of the Air in 1930 with a prominent professor from Columbia University's Teachers College as its chief advisor; and the Mutual Broadcasting System, founded a little later in 1934, organized the Nation's School of the Air series, a somewhat less ambitious commercial educational service (Atkinson, 1938). Despite the effusive rhetoric about their zest for educational quality, and the importance of radio education and radio access for all, NBC and the other commercial networks were well aware that their educational programming, at least during the early days of radio broadcasting, *was* profitable. Having studied the size and distribution of this audience and its proclivity for buying products advertised over the air, the radio industry had found that the profits did not come because students necessarily responded to radio advertising—the youth market was not fully cultivated in the United States until the 1950s. Rather, profits stemmed from ads reaching homemakers and other people who tuned in as they worked at home.

Educators Divide over Commercial Radio

Despite the success of the *Damrosch Hour* and other commercial educational broadcasts, educators became increasingly divided over the future of educational radio. Some were horrified at the idea of corporate-controlled radio. A basic societal mistrust toward big business—the same mistrust evident toward commercialized educational films—was especially apparent with radio, the "true" democratic medium (Fones-Wolf, 1994). Those educators who understood the benefits of noncommercial educational radio and were witness to its increasing (if not alarming) erosion as commercial interests grew more powerful, vigorously opposed commercially based educational content in schools. They believed that ads were not acceptable in the educational arena, that a corporate-sponsored radio curriculum would inherently favor commercial interests, that educational radio would never generate enough profits to satisfy commercial objectives, and that industry control over educational radio would eventually mean the end of all educational radio. These educators—many coming from leading educational organizations—formed an advocacy group in 1930, the National Committee on Educational Radio (NCER), which began to develop a nationwide campaign against commercial broadcasting and promote legislation that would preserve 15% of the radio dial for noncommercial educational content. This move naturally alarmed commercial broadcasters, who were intent on protecting the significant gains they had already made in controlling the radio airwaves and the standardization of advertising practices in the education market. NCER's chairman, Joy Elmer Morgan, relentlessly attacked the radio industry's profit motive:

> As a result of radio broadcasting, there will probably develop during the twentieth century either chaos or a world-order of civilization. Whether it shall be one or the other will depend largely upon whether broadcasting be used as a tool of education or as an instrument of selfish greed. So far, our American radio interests have thrown their major influence on the side of greed. . . . There has never been in the entire history of the United States an example of mismanagement and lack of vision so colossal and far-reaching in its consequences as our turning of the radio channels almost exclusively into commercial hands (quoted in McChesney, 1994, pp. 48–49).

Other educators could not imagine this doomsday scenario. They had a basic trust in commercial broadcasters serving the needs of education. By forming the National Advisory Council on Radio in Education (NACRE), they hoped to work with commercial stations and continue to develop high-quality educational content. They believed that taxpayers would never support a publicly funded network; that commercialized content was the only (and not such a bad) alternative; and that commercial broadcasters would always make room for educational radio in their programming lineup, as long as it met high standards. NACRE's main aim was to promote good relations between educators and the radio industry and to find ways to further collaborate on high-quality educational programs. The educators who most staunchly supported NACRE had in fact been hired by commercial stations or one of the networks to develop programs or act as talent and, not surprisingly, had a stake in advocating more of these kinds of collaborations (see, for example, Gordon, 1942). NACRE's opposition to ads in commercial educational programming—one area where the organization would not cooperate with the industry—gave them a veneer of neutrality. Consequently, numerous teachers took their side. Despite NACRE's anti-ads stance, however, the organization was very much an arm of the radio industry, which praised the council relentlessly for its liaison efforts while lambasting NCER as loony and extreme.

Commercial Radio Has the Last Word

The period between 1928 and 1930 proved to be an active and volatile one for educational radio as the two oppositional educational-radio organizations, NCER and NACRE, vied for influence and as commercial networks grew stronger and more entrenched. In fact, the entire country was divided over the future of radio and there was a growing distaste for advertising on all programs. "It is ridiculous that into 12 million homes should come, for several hours each evening, information and amusement dictated by the manufacturers of toothpaste, . . . and gasoline, and circumscribed both by their intellectual limitations and their greed," the *New Republic* printed in 1930. "Broadly speaking, radio in America is going to waste" (*Education*, p. 135). Even the Federal Radio Commission chairman, Harold A. Lafount, warned his industry in 1931 that commercialized radio would go too far, offending people to the point of revolt (McChesney, 1994). In 1933, the year's national high school debate topic actually asked students to argue either in favor of the publicly funded British Broadcasting Corporation (BBC) model or the "American" commercially dominated alternative (Spring, 1997). Thousands of teenagers across the country were thus researching the benefits and pitfalls of commercially sponsored radio. The broadcasting industry fought back against these (and other) assaults in 1933 by airing weekly "Short Talks on Advertising." Produced by the Advertising Federation of America, the programs were meant to highlight the important attributes of American advertising as a means for bringing happiness and democracy to American citizens (see McChesney, 1994).

Meanwhile, the networks' success at selling ads meant more ads creeping into educational programming. This ad creep angered the listening public, and ads in *education* especially epitomized the evils of the free enterprise system. To avoid public anger over ads in their educational programming, the networks slowly began to reduce their educational offerings. As such, commercial stations were caught up in their own hypocrisy. Because the radio networks had so enthusiastically celebrated the potential of (and their commitment to) radio education, backing out of educational programs caused considerable disfavor among the public and public officials, who had bought into the value of high-quality cultural and educational content. Radio was supposed to bring in real world experts, transmit Harvard-level lectures to the farthest corners of America, and promote widespread democracy, or so Americans were told. The industry was caught in an act of deception.

NCER challenged the radio industry all the way to Capitol Hill. In 1931, Senator Simeon D. Fess (Republican, from Ohio) introduced a bill requesting that 15% of radio's channels be reserved for educational institutions. The 1931 congressional session ended before any action was taken. Three years later, however, in 1934, during a realignment of all radio legislation, the Wagner-Hatfield Amendment was introduced—a bill arguing that 25% of all broadcasting licenses be given to nonprofit stations (Balas, 1999). Many members of Congress were moved to keep the public airwaves public (Hill, 1942). However, the commercial broadcasters were prepared for battle and had been busy between 1931 and 1934 organizing and lobbying against reform legislation. In a stunning moment of history that would have ramifications for all U.S. media for years to come, the radio industry effectively argued a number of positions during the 1934 hearings:

- First, by equating Americanism with democracy, democracy with the free market, and the free market with capitalism, the radio industry linked democracy with capitalism (and a commercial broadcasting system), and proceeded to position the interests of education (as well as religion and other nonprofit interests) as "special interests." With limited frequencies on the AM radio band, there was no room, they argued, for special interests (McChesney, 1994).

- Second, the fact that educators were not united on the role of publicly funded radio education allowed the radio industry to convincingly portray the broadcast-reform effort as fractious and misguided (Saettler, 1990).
- Third, they effectively laid out the position they had maintained since the beginning: Educators at nonprofit stations would never be able to produce high-quality content because American taxpayers would never foot the bill.

Twenty-four days were devoted to these hearings. Out of this time allotment, the NCER had only 10 hours in which to defend their position. "The remainder of time," Hill writes, "was used in hearing the network representatives, the National Association of Broadcasters (NAB), various other commercial radio representatives, spokesmen for labor and religion, and many educators not associated with the [NCER] committee" (1942, p. 70). Indeed, some educators spoke against the 25% allocation, saying that education wasn't ready for such responsibility; others reported cooperative and successful arrangements with the commercial broadcasters. In the end, Congress decided that the entire matter needed more study, so they established the Federal Radio Education Committee, allocating $75,000 in 1935 (Studebaker, 1936), and $130,000 in 1936 (Hill, 1942). Forming a commission to study radio education only gave the networks more time to consolidate their power, and it put the concept of a tax-supported educational network on hold. The landmark 1934 Communications Act was passed without the Wagner-Hatfield Amendment ever becoming a reality.

During this period of increasing corporate control, radio executives and their political supporters continued to speak a high-minded educational rhetoric about the importance of educational radio. At the first National Conference on Educational Broadcasting in 1936, commercial broadcasters (who dominated the conference) linked educational radio to democracy and as a means for vitalizing instruction and as a medium for lifelong learning (Sarnoff, 1936). But these executives also argued that advertising was necessary for the survival of educational radio; that educational radio programs needed to be much better if people were to listen in; and that "educational content" could really be found in nearly every kind of programming they produced.

That same year, the Federal Communications Commission (FCC) asked each licensed station on its renewal form to indicate the time they allotted for educational, agricultural, fraternal, religious, and entertainment purposes. Since none of these terms were defined, however, it was up to the station to determine what counted as educational and other content. The new industry goal, it was clear, was to dismantle educational radio by claiming that all shows could be judged educational. This position justified cutting educational radio—the kind directed toward students—out of the program lineup for good. Indeed, this is exactly what happened. Educational programming began to diminish in the late 1930s and was nearly nonexistent by the mid-1940s. In 1933, CBS had carried 4 educational children's programs and NBC had carried 10. By 1942, CBS had only 1, and NBC had none (Gordon, 1942). That same year, the NCER was dismantled. Its final *Education by Radio* newsletter discussed the many goals the organization had met, including higher-quality radio content. In fact, NCER's biggest concern about a monopoly of radio communication and the not-to-be-trusted interests of the radio industry had been realized. The democratic potential of radio, in education and as a thriving public sphere for the discussion of multiple viewpoints, was gone for good. The reasons, once again, had nothing to do with the technology itself. Teachers had embraced the medium as they had none other before it. But commercial enterprise took control of the medium; educational content interfered with industry profits, and the content was removed, once and for all.

TELEVISION IN THE CLASSROOM

During the 1950s and 1960s, television became another media technology celebrated for its pedagogical promise. Once again, the familiar litany of educational claims accompanied the new medium; according to Levenson and Stasheff (1952), "Television's 'potential' for education was even more loudly proclaimed by educators, manufacturers and broadcasters than that of radio or film" (p. 42). Television would bring in real-world experts, motivate student learning, end educational isolation, and encourage greater democracy. "Students in today's classrooms can be eyewitnesses to history in the making," the Ford Foundation proclaimed in 1961. "They can see and hear the outstanding scholars of our age. They can have access to the great museums of art, history, and nature. A whole treasure-trove of new and stimulating experiences that were beyond the reach of yesterday's students can be brought into the classroom for today's students" (quoted in McKibben, 1992, p. 204). The author of a 1963 *Saturday Evening Post* article describing a French class indicated that televised instruction was an effective teaching method:

> Teaching by television "works"—nobody who has watched a class of children involved with the televised image of Mrs. Ann Slack can have any doubts on the matter. "Ecoutez!" says the pretty Mrs. Slack, pointing the first finger of her left hand to her ear, and the children listen while she says a phrase in French. Then, "Repetez!" says Mrs. Slack, pointing through the set at the children, and they parrot back, but with a surprisingly good accent, what she has said. Children watching a television set in an elementary classroom do not sit limp with slack jaws as they do when they watch a television set at home; they respond with motions and words to what a good teacher on the screen asks them to do. (Mayer, 1963, p. 31)

The writer continued to say, however, that Mrs. Slack was an exception to the norm and that most of the available televised instruction was hopelessly bad. "Educational television has failed to contribute anything important to our schools for one simple reason," the *Post* writer said. "Most of it [the programming] is terrible" (p. 33).

The first problem plaguing educational television was that it was almost nonexistent. Broadcast television as a public medium had been modeled after radio—corporate controlled and advertising supported. Commercial broadcasters were quickly grabbing up television licenses as soon as channels came open, and the Federal Communications Commission (FCC) made no effort to reserve any channels for educational purposes. Because those running these stations were solely interested in making their programs profitable, they invested in easy-to-produce entertainment that satisfied the largest number of people at the lowest possible cost.

Since the television industry had appropriated most of radio's entertainment fare—soap operas, dramas, quiz shows, sports, and so on—educational broadcasting was mostly a dim memory from radio days: a headache and not worth the bother. Consequently, television was, like film, a medium that was commercialized *before* it was considered educational. And, unlike in film, members from the television industry made no attempt to tap into any so-called educational market.

In 1949, however, educational television suddenly got a high-profile advocate in Freida Hennock, one of the seven FCC commissioners, and the commission's lone educational voice (see Balas, 1999). Through Hennock's efforts, a group called the Joint Commission on Educational Television (JCET) was formed, with the aim of reclaiming part of the television spectrum for educational programming. JCET's relative success came from a study it commissioned on the current state of commercial television. A University of Chicago sociologist watched television for 12 straight hours and found no inkling of educational programming whatsoever. His findings were presented at an FCC hearing on educational TV in 1952 and were reinforced by 71 out of the 76 witnesses present (the remaining 5 supported commercial television interests). Shortly after the hearing, the FCC reserved 252 television channels for education and, in so doing, energized an educational television movement across the country. State legislatures provided construction funds for building stations; universities, colleges, and public schools came on board and supplied additional funds; organizational committees began to plan the stations and eventual programming, and national foundations explored the potential of educational television. In Saettler's (1990) words, "The history of educational broadcasting in the United States had entered a new era" (p. 362).

This new era was filled with hopes and pitfalls. Once the new educational stations were in place, barely any funding was available to support adequate material. As a visual medium, television had a far more complicated set of variables involved in its production than did radio, or even film. To pull off a single production, an educational station needed camera operators; audio engineers; set and lighting designers; engineers; makeup and costume personnel; and studio coordination among a host of producers, floor directors, control room directors, and talent. According to Saettler, programs that actually made it to broadcast were infrequently aired and placed in irregular time slots. Some programming was thrown together a few hours before it was broadcast. Not surprisingly, commercial television broadcasters (who coveted the newly built educational stations) began to criticize the efforts behind educational television. An influx of new money from the Ford Foundation—$70 million between 1955 and

1965—was an attempt at remedying the sad state of educational television program content (Saettler, 1990). In 1962 the Kennedy administration apportioned another $32 million for educational television station construction, even though building new stations would not necessarily help program content. Finally, the Johnson administration put the Carnegie Corporation in charge of a study to determine the proper function of educational television. The report's findings—that noncommercial instructional television would be ineffective unless it had higher production values, a broader reach, and a new set of objectives—led to the Public Broadcasting Act of 1967 and the establishment of public television (Balas, 1999).

The battle to create the Public Broadcasting Service (PBS) network was a difficult one. Even as advocates, backed by President Johnson, envisioned a sustainable public resource in public television, the institution was compromised from the beginning. Shaped to disseminate "higher culture" values rather than a diverse range of discourse and aimed at serving the "less attractive" audiences—the over-50 viewer and viewers under 12 (which at that time, anyway, were not valued by advertisers)—PBS created a legacy of educational shows such as *Sesame Street* and *The Electric Company*. The programs were not meant for classroom use. With most of the educational stations becoming PBS affiliates, educational television directed toward the classroom was over.

Videotaped television content, however, began to thrive as an educational supplement beginning in the late 1970s, when videocassette recorder/players entered the consumer market. By the late 1980s, VCRs became a standard addition to many American classrooms and teachers' living rooms. Teachers interested in complementing their instruction with videotaped examples from commercial or PBS television programs could easily tape programs at home, preview particularly helpful sections, and present the material in class as needed. With the additional ability to fast-forward through commercials, pause the tape for discussion, and view it at another point and time (copyrights depending) teachers had a significant amount of control over the technology. Indeed, as cable television offered more and more niche markets, including history, travel (geography), news documentary, movie, and nature channels, teachers had more material to choose from, affording them even more control over the often excellent television fare.

Cable television even encouraged teacher videotaping with the launch of Cable in the Classroom in 1989. The initiative provided public and private schools in the United States with a cable hookup, cable television service and a subscription to the *Cable in the Classroom* newsletter, a listing of programs from cable that can be adapted to classroom use (e.g., A&E's *Biography*, ESPN2's *SportsFigures*, the Weather Channel's *Weather Classroom*). Besides the hookup expenses, the effort did not cost the cable industry much, because the programs listed were already produced for existing cable networks. Indeed, since teachers had already established the practice of videotaping cable programs, the Cable in the Classroom initiative more or less legitimized the practice. The industry accommodated teachers further by providing commercial-free versions of specific education-oriented listings in early-morning slots so that teachers could tape uninterrupted versions of the shows and use them in class.

Responsible, sponsor-free television content had arrived for classroom use. But as usual, there was a catch. Schools were still responsible for funding the video equipment and some of the cable service fees and cable guides—in New York State alone this cost would amount to $1 million annually (Sanger, 1990). Much of the listed programming—for example, *Scooby Doo: The Headless Horseman of Halloween*, which was recommended for classroom showing around Halloween—was also clearly aimed at generating larger audiences for established cable fare and network brands. "Our business motivation is always to increase the value of the network," A&E Network spokesperson Dan Davids said in 1990. "If viewers enjoy 'A&E Classroom,' the educational segment, they also may watch other shows on the network, which carries advertising. And the more viewers that like a network, the greater incentive cable operators have to carry it" (Sanger, 1990, p. 2).

Since franchises require cable companies to demonstrate that they are responsive to community needs, a cable company's involvement in local educational efforts signals community philanthropy and better ensures the company's contract renewal. Cable programmers also have an incentive to create programming that can be slotted into an educational setting in order to enhance their image and better secure a place on the cable lineup. Finally, any industry efforts to cater to education look good to members of Congress, who determine cable legislation.

It was the usefulness and familiarity of video technology that prompted many schools to accept Channel One in their classrooms. Established in 1989 by Chris Whittle of Whittle Communications, Channel One is an ad-supported, 12-minute news program sent via satellite to participating schools. Those schools that participate must require their students to watch the daily program and its accompanying commercials (for such products as Coke, Reebok, Hostess Twinkies, and Clearasil) in order to receive in return a videocassette recorder and television monitor for every classroom. The deal has proved so tempting among school administrators hoping to save money on VCR equipment that by 2003, 40% of American secondary schools required their students to watch Channel One broadcasts.

Channel One created a new era of educational television. Besides promoting the necessity of video technology in the classroom, the company won over administrators and educators on its educational television format: slick, student-friendly broadcasts that were sold as a necessary and important way to educate students about world events. In a widely quoted justification during the early years of Channel One, Whittle reportedly argued that students were mixing up Cher and Chernobyl—an obvious indication that they were significantly lacking in news knowledge. Channel One was supposed to remedy these ills. The president of Teenage Research Unlimited, Peter Zollo, would reinforce this point in his book, *Wise Up to Teens: Insights into Marketing and Advertising to Teenagers* (1995). Speaking for his company, Zollo writes:

> Our position is that Channel One is sound programming. It makes news relevant to kids. Its coverage of the fall of the Berlin Wall, for example, opened the eyes of thousands of American teens. Furthermore, teens are bombarded with hundreds of advertising messages every day. Because advertising has become so much a part of their lives, they are quite adept at tuning it in or out. To some, this point alone might not justify in-school TV advertising, but in combination with the quality of the program, we feel comfortable recommending Channel One to advertisers. Another plus for the schools is that Channel One gives VCRs and televisions to schools that air its programming. (p. 83)

Unlike in the case of broadcast and cable television content taped at home and brought into school, however, teachers have no control over Channel One satellite transmissions—they are required to turn on the 12-minute program each day and keep the volume knob at an audible level. The Channel One agreement also requires that 90% of a school's student body watch the broadcast each day.

At the onset of Channel One's broadcast initiative, a large number of teachers and parents protested the program and called the equipment-for-student-attention arrangement blackmail. Indeed, with an increasing amount of corporate-sponsored curriculum material entering the classroom since World War II, which accelerated all the more during the 1980s and 1990s, Channel One prompted the most explosive anticorporate response among teachers since the radio era (Molnar, 1996). Most of the protests against Channel One have concerned the 2 minutes of advertising content accompanying each program. Other critics have noted that 42% of the 12-minute "educational" broadcast amounts to filler, such as promotional content and teasers for upcoming stories (Alexander & Dichter, 2000).

Despite Channel One's commercials and questionable news content and the company's overall business motive, many teachers and students in Channel One schools are simply resigned to its daily presence. The Channel One program thrives in schools for a variety of specific reasons not connected to any curriculum choices: the decision to bring not just the technology, but a specific *program,* into schools, is made at the administrative, not the teacher, level. (In some cases, complaints from teachers may indeed jeopardize their relationship with administrators). Students therefore watch the program as part of a contract, not a teacher decision. Keeping the technology working is in the best interest of Channel One, so teachers are not responsible for its upkeep. Consequently, "the technology" is not an issue in Channel One's implementation. The administrators, teachers, and students who find value in the program are also part of a new generation of Americans who are less concerned about commercialized content. Furthermore, the program, which usually plays during homeroom at the beginning of a school day, stays outside teachers' individual curriculum content, reducing its pedagogical utility, but also teacher resistance to the program.

Other teachers actually welcome Channel One, because it offers them 12 free minutes in the beginning of a very busy day: Many use the time to organize their teaching materials. On rare occasions, some teachers counter Channel One's message by introducing media-literacy skills during the broadcasts. The majority of students, according to researcher Roy Fox (1996), are also more interested in the entertainment value of Channel One and actually prefer the "fun" advertising content over the more boring news content. "Most students I talked with found many ways to embrace commercials, to trust them, to view advertisers' motives in a positive, trusting way," he wrote (p. 2). This response, of course, is a significant shift from the situation in the 1930s, when the general consensus among educators and their students was that corporate-sponsored messages necessarily tainted classroom objectives.

In explaining the attitude shift between the 1930s and 1980s, Fones-Wolf (1994) notes that after World War II, the business community aimed at changing these "un-American" attitudes by bringing "a new intensity and sophistication to the task of influencing children" (p. 203). Business gifts to schools amounted to $24 million in 1948 and skyrocketed to $280 million in 1965; the business community manufactured educational crises during the 1950s (and later during the 1980s) and proceeded to "rescue" public schools, while drawing attention to their corporate activities and donations; corporations also brought teachers and students to production centers and manufacturing plants (see Molnar, 1996); they successfully lobbied for economics and business classes (pp. 194–204); and they created increasingly sophisticated teacher aids and curriculum materials (often enlisting teachers in their production). Fones-Wolf provides this interesting data:

> In 1950, the National Association of Manufacturers [NAM] alone distributed almost 4.5 million pamphlets to students, representing a 600% increase over 1947. It also doubled school usage of its films between 1947 and 1949; by 1954 over 3.5 million students watched about 60,000 showings of NAM films. That year, school superintendents estimated that the investment in free material at $50 million, about half the amount public schools spent annually on regular textbooks. At the end of the decade, one in five corporations reported supplying teaching aids. (1994, p. 204)

Since teachers' unions, at the time, were more focused on immediate political and economic struggles, they did not provide opposition to this longer-term ideological movement. Fones-Wolf (1994) has articulated how the business community was so successful in altering the public's perception of business that it had a free hand in schools by the early 1960s. Many teachers and students had been successfully "indoctrinated" with "an economic interpretation that taught that the American economy was 'free, competitive, and individualistic' and must be retained without change" (p. 211).

Both commercialized radio and television also worked as ideological apparatuses for the general public. As Kellner (1990) observed, television was crucial in the post–World War II boom period, "because its advertisements promoted consumption and its programs celebrated the joys of the consumer society" (p. 42). Accordingly, Americans have now become inured to nearly 80 years of advertising on radio and television, and teachers have come to expect an invasion of corporate sponsorship and values into their schools (Fox, 1996; Molnar, 1996).

Since the 1930s there has been another corresponding economic shift making it sensible for companies to place educational television programs (and other sponsored materials) in schools: The rise of the American youth culture in the 1950s after World War II created a deluge of teen-directed fashions, music, movies, television shows, and promotions for big-ticket-item products such as stereos and cars. In order to participate in this new culture, more and more young people entered the job market, became consumers themselves, began to increasingly influence their parents' purchases at increasingly younger ages, and came to be recognized as important trendsetters who would be spending even more money in the future. The pace of teenage consumption dramatically picked up during the 1980s (the same time that Channel One was developed) and again in the 1990s (Alexander & Dichter, 2000). Thus, marketing to teens via the media today is in great contrast to what occurred in the 1930s, when radio broadcasters chose to overlook children in schools and instead target the mothers listening at home. As teenage-marketing strategist Peter Zollo (1995) put it, "The stereotype of today's teen is a brand-obsessed, label-driven, mall-congregating, free-spending, compulsive shopper. There is often some truth to stereotypes" (p. 22). From a business perspective, then, marketing to teenagers in school, where they are a captive audience, is desirable and profitable, especially when educator concern over commercialism is minimal. Community leaders, according to Alex Molnar (1996), rarely voice ethical or educational objections to school-based marketing and cast these "partnerships" as beneficial to all parties involved (p. 25).

Broadcast television as an educational technology has thus found its way into the classroom. While the broadcasts are not necessarily successful from an educational perspective, they most certainly are so from an economic perspective. The Channel One audience is 50 times the size of MTV's teen audience (Alexander & Dichter, 2000). By targeting ads to teens as effectively as the Super Bowl targets men, Channel One's corporate owner, magazine conglomerate PRIMEDIA, generates $800,000 a day on just 2 minutes of ads—at advertising rates rivaling those of prime-time television shows (Hays, 1999). Not surprisingly, PRIMEDIA calls itself "the leading targeted media company" that offers "highly effective advertising and marketing solutions in some of the most sought after niche markets."

HISTORY LESSONS FOR THE INTERNET

In reviewing the history of the educational-technology industries (and the educational content that came out of these industries), it is clear that teachers were concerned about—and constrained by—their ability to produce or influence educational content. Unable to control content, which inevitably became limited and commercialized by a for-profit agenda, teachers rejected it and the educational technologies it was played on.

In the case of film, the commercial educational-film industry controlled all aspects of film content, except in the few cases when educators acted as advisors in a particular film series. High-quality film content was too expensive and difficult to create given the nature of film production, and most of the available educational films were industry afterthoughts, typically bad, and rejected by teachers. Government extension services solved some access problems (while creating others) but did not solve the problem of the quality of available films. Consequently, the content—and its accompanying technology—was not successful in schools.

In the case of radio, teachers had a considerable amount of control over radio content early on, and they were vigorously supportive of radio production and radio technology as a publicly owned medium. Given the political and economic context of the 1930s and 1940s, however, and the potential of radio as an advertising-supported mass medium, educators' initial control was eventually usurped by an increasingly powerful radio industry. With a potent radio lobby (and the ensuing discord among educators), Congress consistently voted in favor of commercial radio. The radio industry also appeased educators by producing quality educational-radio content—with educators' help—during a short but optimistic period. The industry's monopoly over public air-

waves, however, meant that commercial broadcasters would eventually choose to broadcast only that material that generated the greatest
profit. Because educational radio programs were decidedly not as profitable for the radio industry as other programs, they disappeared altogether, and as a consequence, radio became less and less useful to
schools. The content disappeared, and so did the technology.

During the early years of television, educational content for
schools was nonexistent, because business interests controlled the
medium. When educational stations were eventually developed (as a
result of significant government and nonprofit initiatives), the nature
of the medium proved too difficult and too expensive for educators to
create valuable educational programs. VCR technology changed that
to a large extent, bringing to classrooms valuable curriculum supplements that had high production values and were significantly under
teachers' control. The cable television industry has successfully
repackaged some of its programming for educational purposes,
allowing teachers control over cable's offerings, but also allowing
more chances for the cable industry to introduce teachers and their
students to its "brands." Channel One, however, does not rely on
teacher acceptance for its success: Its presence is brought about by
administrators, not teachers. Channel One, the commercially charged
in-school broadcast of our current era, is economically, not pedagogically, successful.

In light of the history of educational media, the central question to
be asked about the future of internet technology is also economic—
namely, Under what auspices should online educational content be
presented—commercial or nonprofit? Given the internet's democratic
structure; its essentially unlimited space; the comparatively low production costs of locating, listing, and organizing web links; and the
ease of producing original pages, will the internet be an educator's
medium? Will educators be, as with the radio era, heavily involved in
(and enthusiastic about) creating pedagogically valuable curriculum
content? Will educators (and others) be critical of corporate-dominat-
ed Net spaces, and incorporate media literacy initiatives into the curriculum to better understand the United States' corporate-controlled
media systems?

Alternately, if internet educational content becomes dominated by
commercial fare that is acceptable to schools and educators, which
happened with radio, will educators be less likely to create nonprofit

alternatives? Will educators become so used to a corporate-sponsored internet environment that ambitious and worthwhile nonprofit ventures get edged out? Will commercial online educational ventures, like Channel One in the educational television sector, successfully harness the youth market for profit and, as such, potentially exploit student users? Will the educational content accessible on the internet become, like educational film, radio, and television, so commercially dominated that it becomes pedagogically compromised?

Finally, even if commercial ventures eventually dominate the online educational scene, will it matter at all if a profit motive, not an educational one, drives webpage access and content? Should we trust that commercial educational portals will work with educators and invest heavily in locating quality links, with a traditional journalistic firewall separating the business and editorial departments? Should we trust that commercial search engines will develop as trustworthy and reliable information services? Should we expect that students will have valuable educational opportunities online, regardless of the internet's commercialization?

CHAPTER 2

Wiring America's Schools

The highway is going to give us all access to seemingly unlimited information, anytime and anyplace we care to use it. It's an exhilarating prospect, because putting this technology to use to improve education will lead to downstream benefits in every area of society.

—Bill Gates, 1995

As we go up to 2000, 2001, we will shift from an investment mode to a return mode, a period when we start getting profits in from this major investment.

—Bill Gates, 1998

The rise of the internet, first as research tool and then as a mass medium, has been faster than any other new communication medium to date. Schools played a large role in this meteoric rise. First sold to North America as the information superhighway, the internet had mass appeal as an educational tool, which was a major factor in accelerating the medium's growth. Because the internet was so closely allied to education in its early years, its rise bears a striking resemblance to that of radio. Like radio, the internet blossomed in educational circles before it became harnessed for commercial purposes. As with radio, educators could easily produce, disseminate, and control content, making it especially appealing to teachers. And as with radio, the intensive efforts of a powerful industry, and a lack of government regulation and investment, have diminished its value as a medium for education. The main difference between radio and the internet is that educators really did control radio for a short period of time before the radio industry got the upper hand. Seventy years later, corporate interests were far more savvy, using educational rhetoric from the outset to more quickly gain control of the new internet medium. This chapter is the story of how this was done.

The internet began in the late 1960s as a military computer network that permitted different people in separate locations to communicate with one another over existing telephone lines. Supported by the U.S. Defense Department's Advanced Research Project Administration (ARPA), researchers at universities and corporations designed a distributed network system that became the ARPANet (or the Net) so that no communication would be routed through a central switcher. The system was ingenious because it avoided communication clogs and could withstand any kind of system errors, natural disasters, or military attacks by quickly finding other paths to route the lines of communication.

During the early years of internet development, only those institutions and universities with defense contracts could use the Net. By the 1970s, however, researchers from nonaffiliated universities began pushing for the ability to exchange data over the network as well. The government thus established two independent networks in the 1970s and 1980s, the Computers and Science Network (CSNET) and the "Because It's Time Network" (BITNET), to be used for academic research. While the Defense Department's desire to continue ARPANet funding decreased during the mid-1980s, the government developed another university research network, NSFNet, based in the National Science Foundation (NSF). NSFNet connected to all interested universities at no cost and to the corporate sector for a fee. The publicly funded NSF also funded five supercomputer sites and high-speed network lines between them. According to Aufderheide (1999), this connection matrix "allowed NSFNET to become the 'backbone' of an entire collection of networks that is known collectively as the Internet" (p. 231).

Between 1988 and 1990, as the government withdrew ARPANet funding entirely, the internet mainly functioned as a university-based network. Academic researchers, computer programmers, and amateur hackers all tinkered away at this new tool of communication, developing news groups, gopher lists, one-to-one email communication, and new ways to pass along large chunks of research data and other information. Like the radio hackers of the 1910s who no longer had to rely on AT&T or the government to transmit communication over vast distances, these inventors—often young researchers at universities—reveled in the internet's democratic, if not anarchic, possibilities. As Burstein and Kline wrote in 1995, "Simply put, the Internet is ungovernable . . . you can pretty much do what you want—and for the most part, there's no sheriff or posse to stop you" (pp. 113–114).

During this experimental phase, with more and more users logging on worldwide, sharing information, and generating excitement about the medium, the internet had become, in Campbell, Martin, and Fabos's (2003) words, "an enormous free-floating library without a Dewey decimal system" (p. 46). Three other developments made the internet more easily accessible during the early 1990s. First, in 1991, Tim Berners-Lee, a researcher at the Geneva-based nuclear research institute Conseil Européen pour la Recherche Nucléaire (CERN) made an enormously important internet contribution by developing hypertext. This development led to the worldwide web, a data-linking system that enabled users to easily skip to related information sources via hypertext links. Second, the National Super Computing Administration (NSCA) at the University of Illinois released the Mosaic browser software, developed in 1993. Mosaic handled the web files and links and translated them into a user-friendly graphic layout. And third, search engine technology helped users find specific sites by means of key words. Consequently, more and more people began developing homepages and sharing in this global information exchange. Educators, especially at the university level, continued to play a large part in developing internet capabilities and in providing and disseminating internet content.

During this early era of web connectivity, the internet again can be likened to radio in that users were not yet able to grasp how the web would ultimately operate beyond a research and communication tool spreading knowledge, democracy, and free speech across cyberspace. In fact, when Al Gore was a senator on the Science Committee in the early 1990s, he framed the internet in terms of its potential value in education, and he proposed the creation of a National Research and Education Network. To his mind, the internet needed to be a government-supported communications medium that highlighted education in function and purpose. In coining the term *information superhighway* in 1992, Gore meant to compare the internet to the publicly supported interstate road network that his father, when a senator, had backed in the 1950s. This governmentally funded educational network would never be established, however. The building excitement over the internet had also reached the corporate sector, which was suddenly under-standing the medium as a valuable extension of existing, corporate-owned telecommunications services. Accordingly, these commercial interests were suddenly determined to control the new medium. They had the power, and certainly a legacy of government-supported tele-phone, radio, and television monopolies, to enlist government sup-port on their behalf. Aufderheide (1999) has documented this impor-tant development:

> As enthusiasm for the concept grew . . . major telecommunications interests became alarmed at the idea of federal investment in and control over aspects of telecommunications service. By the time Clinton took office, it was firmly established that the information superhighway would be a private-sector initiative with government encouragement. (p. 43)

As with radio, then, the internet's potential as a commercial medi-um developed alongside its potential as an educational tool. Education would have a particularly important function, however, in popularizing the internet toward commercial ends.

A HAIRPIN TURN ON THE INFORMATION SUPERHIGHWAY: 1993–1995

By 1993, technology developments enabled internet users to transmit pictures, sounds, and video files, bringing on a new era of multimedia and digital convergence. It was at about this time that the internet began appearing in public schools. K–12 educators were increasingly enthused about this "living" textbook and communication tool and about the ways it could be applied in the classroom. Students could access streams of free educational material and countless discussions on controversial topics with wide-ranging viewpoints. They could learn how to mine vast data banks, learn information-discrimination techniques, and write reports using up-to-date facts. Unlike all the classroom technologies before it, the internet also afforded interactiv-ity: Experts could write or talk back to answer student queries—even in real time—and schools could connect with other teachers and stu-dents around the world. Some technologically adept teachers began sharing internet resources with other teachers, creating their own internet environments, learning, along with their students, how to develop homepages and disseminate student writing, research projects, artwork, and other useful class materials over the web. Likewise, librarians began to catalog websites they deemed to have exceptional informational value.

Here was an educational technology, like radio, that could enable educators to link to existing content outside the classroom *and* to produce educational content relatively cheaply after the initial technological investments were made. With its ability to transmit information about school and classroom activities and accommodate email questions from parents, the internet could also be an exciting means for peer interaction and homework help outside class, as well as a means for greater parental involvement, an issue of increasing importance among educators.

Here was a technology that could also allow teachers an unprecedented amount of choice, flexibility, and control over what content to bring into the classroom and *when*; they could access any part of the internet at any time. Indeed, besides being a research tool and "real-life" textbook, the internet was a writing lab, a conversation and debate forum, a student/teacher portfolio, and a wide-reaching educational community, 24 hours a day. As such, the "library" of internet content itself could be conveniently reached from a student's home (as long as there was a connection). Early educational "how-to" books appeared in 1993, including *The Internet in K–12 Education* and *Libraries and the Internet*, which outlined the internet's possibilities for schools and universities. Meanwhile, the term *information superhighway* was becoming the label for a common way to think about the internet in the popular media. News reports suggested that the internet would bring amazing home, work, and school conveniences, which would lead to copious learning activities. Other reports dwelled on the comfortable online shopping opportunities for people who preferred to peruse the web late at night in their pajamas; the potential of the internet's 500 TV channel capacity; and a new range of telecommunications services that would lead to cheaper phone bills.

In 1993, the Clinton administration introduced the public service www.whitehouse.gov, which allowed citizens to access government databases and webpages containing material regarding history, policy, and communications. This website was meant to illustrate the internet's democratic spirit: With direct access to government databases and White House speeches, the public could be more involved in government decision-making. As the news media exalted whitehouse.gov, the White House much more quietly released a series of business-related reports having to do with internet technology and economic growth. The first report, called "Technology for Economic Growth in America," discussed the growing importance of information technology in terms of U.S. economic expansion. "American technology must move in a new direction to build economic strength and spur economic growth," it read ("Technology," 1993). The second report, "Building a Stronger, Hi-Tech, Deregulated Economy," released a month later, called for the development of a nationwide "superhighway" ("Building," 1993) and discussed the internet's potential as a means for greater business efficiency. Again identifying the internet as the "engine of economic growth," the report advised that the government should make the acceleration of the "National Information Infrastructure" of high-speed telecommunications networks, advanced computer systems, and software a top priority ("Reengineering," 1993).

Ultimately, corporate interests saw this government interest and involvement in the e-commerce infrastructure as threatening to their plans to control internet commerce. As one telecommunications executive wrote in a public letter to *USA Today*'s business section at the end of 1993:

> I'm glad to hear Al Gore and the administration are active supporters of the information superhighway. I am concerned, however, about the level of government involvement they have in mind. Many industry insiders agree government should ease restrictions. But it should limit its involvement. Too much government involvement, and the wish of many to make access to the superhighway free to all, will be as counterproductive as the outdated restrictions they want to lift. When I speak to groups about the information highway, the audience is always supportive of the free market and competitive forces being allowed to operate in order to allow the superhighway to reach its full potential. Let's face it; if it weren't for the old-fashioned profit motive, cable TV would be but a mere shadow of its present self. Let the free market work. (December 28, p. 8A).

The Clinton administration, having a desire to move forward on the information superhighway but experiencing intense pressure from lobbyists, a Republican-controlled House of Representatives, and other allies within the corporate sector, deferred to the telecommunications and cable industry's hunger for control over the internet. Subsequently, the Clinton administration endorsed a philosophy of commercial internet, similar to the governments' "philosophy of commercial radio" established in the 1930s. In a move that would ripple through the media industry in years to come, the Clinton administration in 1993 proposed deregulation legislation that evolved into the landmark Telecommunication Act of 1996. During this period of the act's development, a few legislators attempted to protect the internet (or elements of it) as a publicly owned space. In 1993, Ed Markey (Democrat, from Massachusetts) and Jack Fields (Republican, from Texas) sponsored H.R. 3636, which, apart from proposing more severe limitations on telephone company ownership, also included the notion of a universal service, price breaks to educational and medical facilities, and government inquiries to promote civic uses of the internet (Aufderheide, 1999, p. 50). When this bill was absorbed into another internet-related bill, H.R. 3626 (rigidly representing telecommunication company interests), H.R. 3636 slid away while H.R. 3626 passed easily. Then a year later, U.S. senators Ernest Hollings (Democrat, from South Carolina) and John Danforth (Republican, from Missouri) sponsored S. 1822, which also advocated universal service and the support of internet access for nonprofit institutions. Significantly, the bill contained an amendment proposed by Sen. Daniel Inouye (Democrat, from Hawaii) that, quite similar to the failed Wagner-Hatfield Amendment to the Communications Act of 1934, asked for 20% of the internet's available space to be reserved for public interest. The bill's 20% set-aside was then reduced to 5%, with provisions to ensure that the internet would accommodate a diverse communication forum:

> The builders of these new networks will use real public property for laying copper wires, coaxial cable, and fiber optic cable, and use previously unused electromagnetic frequencies. The public has a right to demand compensations to the form of public access to such networks by entities that provide substantial benefits to the public. . . . Second, the U.S. Government has a compelling interest in ensuring that all citizens of the United States have access to a broad and diverse array of communications services, including noncommercial educational, informational, cultural, civic, and charitable services. Such broad access furthers the Government's compelling interests in education, in facilitating widespread public discourse among all citizens, and in improving democratic self-governance. Because citizens now receive a large majority of their information through use of these telecom-

munications networks, the owners of these networks will become gatekeepers of the information that the public receives. . . . Third, the owners of these telecommunications networks are likely to design their networks so as to maximize the potential profit of such networks. . . . These owners are unlikely to adopt rate structures that will allow access for entities with few financial resources. In particular, entities providing noncommercial educational, informational, cultural, civic, and charitable services are likely to be excluded. . . . By reserving capacity for public users, the legislation provides a public forum for speech without involving the Government in regulating speech content. (United States Congress, Senate, Committee on Commerce, Science, and Transportation, quoted in Aufderheide, 1999, p. 52).

According to Aufderheide (1999), the bill made a remarkable statement about the need to create a public sphere in cyberspace. "It was especially noteworthy," she writes, "because it employed the notion of 'the public' in a way that did not simply equate the public with competition and consumer price and new-product benefits" (p. 52). Unlike what occurred during the 1934 debates about the future of radio as a public medium (see Balas, 1999), the concept of the internet as a universally accessible public sphere did not become a public issue, mostly because the U.S. media, dominated by the same commercial forces, failed to cover it. The bill quietly died before it ever reached the floor of the Senate. Other bills cast the internet according to the interests of the telephone and cable industry and the Republican leadership. Even as nonprofits, including the Center for Media Education, the Media Access Project, the Benton Foundation, and the National Education Association, attempted to revive the 5% set-aside of S. 1822, these efforts were easily stamped out in the highly politicized and deregulation-friendly 104th Congress (Aufderheide, 1999). Commerce, not education, would have its way.

In 1994, more internet developments pointed to the web as a future venue for commercial enterprise. For starters, Netscape, a commercial version of the Mosaic browser software, became available and proved to be immediately successful—much more so than its precursor. Through Netscape, the first searchable shopping malls emerged on the web, allowing users to experience the web as an electronic catalog or store. Furthermore, new marketing research indicated that the internet had tremendous and novel advertising and marketing potential, as well as being an effective means for the direct distribution of certain goods. These initial studies found that the internet, when used properly, could target appealing demographics (e.g., people in the 16–34 age range) and reach individuals more effectively and cheaply than traditional advertising strategies.

Not surprisingly, sponsored websites were anathema to the internet's original users (or "netizens," as they were called at the time), who gasped at the banner ads and email-based marketing strategies appearing on the web and invading their public space. As *Business Week* published in 1994:

> Advertising on the Internet. Just a few months ago, the very idea caused Internet veterans to gnash their teeth. The Internet community had thrived—both socially and technically—precisely because of its implicit ethic: Give as much as you take. Where else could a university researcher, say, offer thousands of colleagues copies of her new database program and then enjoy a flood of comments and improvements in return—at essentially no charge to anyone? Madison Avenue, with its one-way messages and penchant for mass market overkill, would seem the very antithesis of the Internet culture. (November 14, p. 84)

Accordingly, marketing researchers advised that commercial enterprises come together to develop new standards for facilitating commerce and devise strategies that would be less offensive. One piece of advice included designing "marketing innovations that take advantage of the medium's inherent interactivity and 'play value,'" and developing "stimulating and exciting content-rich sponsored environments" (Hoffman, 1995, p. 2). Not surprisingly, another 1994 development was CommerceNet, an organization committed to transforming the internet into a global electronic marketplace. "Stop thinking about it as the Information Highway and start thinking about it as the marketing superhighway," Don Logan, president and CEO of Time, Inc., said to the Association of National Advertisers during this period. "Doesn't it sound better already?" (Burstein & Kline, 1995, p. 101).

The year 1995 would be pivotal in terms of the way the internet began to be framed in both private and public arenas. First of all, the online dial-up systems America Online, Compuserve, and Prodigy took off in the home market; more home users were logging on, joining chat groups, creating their own homepages, and exploring the already existing internet content. Second, Microsoft released its

Windows 95 operating system, which was bundled with the company's internet browser, Microsoft Explorer. The release was a major event for the computer industry, driving holiday computer and software sales. Third, an investment frenzy over internet stock—as evidenced by Netscape's initial public offering (IPO) of its stock—brought to a new level internet entrepreneurialism, the growth of the web, and internet market expectations. And fourth, and perhaps most important, control of the high-speed NSFNet lines, which had been maintained by the government since 1986 and were considered the backbone of the internet, was silently transferred to cable and local phone companies, effectively ending direct government involvement in the internet (see Aufderheide, 1999). There was little debate on this business-friendly transfer because the news media was steered in other directions, as I will illustrate below.

The developments between 1993 and 1995 set the internet on a course as a medium for increased electronic commerce ("Ready," 1994). Yet, beginning in 1995, the rhetoric of government officials as well as that of corporate advertising and public relations efforts emphasized an entirely different use for the internet—as an educational tool. Indeed, for 3 years, images of internet education flooded the news media. Consequently, the most popular way to understand the internet as a new, exciting, and transformative technology, was that it was a conduit for education. These strategic corporate and political messages belied Washington's quiet efforts to prioritize the internet and make it the centerpiece of the nation's commercial activity.

THE EDUCATIONAL "CHALLENGE": 1995–1998

On September 21, 1995, President Clinton gave a pivotal speech to elementary school students, government officials, and a number of executives from information companies, who were all gathered in the rotunda of San Francisco's Exploratorium, the city's hands-on "museum of science, art, and human perception." The setting was symbolic: San Francisco is the home of "internet row," the growing center of much online activity; and California, the home to Silicon Valley, is the most technologically innovative state in the nation.

It was here that Clinton issued his first "challenge" to America "to see to it that every classroom in our country is connected to the Information Superhighway." Speaking about the "vast world of knowledge" available through the internet and about the need to get American children hooked "not on tobacco but on education," President Clinton validated education, rather than commerce, as the most important aspect of the internet. Indeed, it seemed as if the Clinton administration was reverting to an earlier 1992 initiative, which would have provided a governmentally controlled, educational network for schools, colleges, and universities. This was not the case, however. Clinton's speech was calculated to enlist private-sector companies—such as AT&T, Sprint, MCI, Pacific Bell, America Online, Sun Microsystems, Apple, Xerox Parc, Oracle, 3com, Silicon Graphics, Applied Materials, TCI, and Cisco Systems (all represented in the Exploratorium audience)—in the school-wiring effort. By asking for their partnership, Clinton was signaling that all internet-related efforts on behalf of education would be, at least in part, within the context of corporate control.

In announcing the California initiative, which would connect all the state's schools to the internet by the end of the year, Clinton introduced the model for a larger, national initiative to wire all of America's schools by 2000:

> If we can connect 20% of the schools in the largest state in the nation in less than a year, we can surely connect the rest of the country by the end of the decade. In the coming days, I will announce the winners of our Technology Learning Challenge. And over the next several weeks, I will put forward a public-private partnership plan that lays out how we can move our entire nation toward the goal of technological literacy for every young person in America.

Clinton noted education technology research studies—which incidentally had been conducted by the computer industry—to justify the absolute need for internet technologies in school. "The facts speak for themselves," he said. "Children with access to computers learn faster and better."

In this education vision, volunteers, not the government, would help the private sector in activating classroom wiring efforts. As Press Secretary Mike McCurry explained after Clinton's address, the administration had been planning this initiative in cooperation with the telecommunications industry. "What we are so excited about here today is that the private sector, which has long had an interest in seeing how they could help California schools, have really come together now in a very specific way and set some goals that they believe are achievable" (McCurry, 1995). Clinton's speech, then, was described as a catalyst to pull telecommunications companies together and, in McCurry's words, a way to "really light a fire to get actual work done" (McCurry, 1995). It was also meant to recognize the work that had already been completed in the California effort, which was framed in terms of philanthropy and public gains. Clinton pointed to a coalition of Silicon Valley companies that had already contributed $15 million toward wiring California's schools; America Online for supplying a year's worth of internet service; AT&T for providing internet access and voice mail; Sprint for providing hookups; MCI for providing software; and Sun Microsystems and Pacific Bell for leading the way in linking schools.

Along with the private sector, Clinton used his speech to challenge community members—parents, students, local officials, and industry professionals—to volunteer their time toward the noble goal of student learning. He highlighted a nonprofit volunteer organization called NetDay, which had been founded earlier that year. Begun by John Gage (from Sun Microsystems) and Michael Kaufman (from the public TV station and PBS affiliate KQED), NetDay facilitated "high-tech barn raisings" (a phrase used by both Clinton and Gore) twice a year, generating community excitement about classroom internet technology, selling comprehensive wiring kits to schools at volume discounts, and tracking the percentage of wired schools. "In the morning," Clinton said, "volunteers will arrive at each school. By noon they will have wired the library, the labs, the classrooms. By nightfall, those schools will have the technology they deserve." Gore, especially, would become a popular figure on NetDays, appearing on local news programs dressed in work clothes and posing inside school corridors on top of stepladders. Such high-profile political involvement in conjunction with rather large scale community efforts inevitably generated positive public relations regarding student internet use.

With this speech, then, internet-enhanced education would become a main theme in Clinton administration rhetoric for the following 3 years. Shortly after the September 1995 address, a number of education-oriented announcements from the White House followed:

- December 1995. An advisory council to President Clinton released a report based on a 2-year study on school internet use that cited "dramatic" results for "at-risk" students, and argued for the importance of "bringing the world's best materials into the classrooms of the nation's worst-off students" ("Connecting," 1995). The council's recommendation: Every community needs to connect its elementary and secondary schools to the internet.

- January 1996. Al Gore unveiled the "Welcome to the White House for Kids" site at a technologically advanced elementary school in San Carlos, California. Users logging on to the site were greeted by Socks, the Clinton family cat, who gave virtual tours of the White House.
- February 1996. Having initially acted to motivate private-sector and community involvement, the Clinton-Gore administration began to commit more government investment toward educational internet access. As part of the Telecommunications Act of 1996, the $2.25 billion E-rate initiative aimed to give 20 to 90% discounts on the telecommunication services needed to wire schools and libraries.
- June 1996. The Department of Education's technology literacy plan called for a $2 billion investment in public schools over 5 years, seed monies to be matched by state, local, industry, and business dollars to meet four goals:

    1. All teachers in the nation will have the training and support they need to help students learn using computers and the information superhighway.
    2. All teachers and students will have modern multimedia computers in their classrooms.
    3. Every classroom will be connected to the information superhighway.
    4. Effective software and online learning resources will be an integral part of every school's curriculum (Riley, 1996).

- February 1997. In his State of the Union address, President Clinton proclaimed that his number-one priority for the following 4 years would be education. Clinton listed a number of traditional issues on which his administration would focus its attention, including standards, literacy, Head Start, school vouchers, building "character," and school repair. Clinton's last point, his educational finale, was his personal push to make the internet accessible to all American schoolchildren (Clinton, 1997b).

These governmental efforts inevitably increased the profile of internet-based education and drew attention to the many educational internet activities that had already been under way.

While the telecommunications and computer industry were no doubt happy about extending their internet-access services to many more users, they were not thrilled with the idea of footing the school and library hook-up bills. Clinton's original plan would have made the telecommunications industry solely responsible for wiring the schools. After they opposed this arrangement, the FCC arranged for a compromise in 1996: The telecommunications industry would now be committed to offering schools and libraries 40–60% discounts off of regular rates; schools in low-income areas would receive up to 90% off. Local and state funding would cover the rest. However, to finance the discounts, computer, telecommunication, and internet-related companies would create an annual $2.25 billion funding pool, which would be generated by taxing citizens' phone bills, thereby fully subsidizing the cost of telecommunication companies' internet services and equipment. U.S. citizens continue to pay a small "E-rate" tax on their phone bills each month to fund the technology discounts.

INTERNET IN THE SCHOOLS:
THE CORPORATE CONNECTION

Even so, other members of the business community quickly saw an opportunity in embracing this new theme of internet-enhanced education, and suddenly began to package online education as the priority of the future web. One of these was Microsoft chairman Bill Gates. Recalling Thomas Edison, with his commercial film interests, or RCA/NBC executive David Sarnoff, who espoused educational rhetoric with regard to radio, Gates was one of a number of corporate elites who exalted the internet's educational promise while having a considerable amount to gain through the internet's widespread acceptance. In November 1995, 2 months after Clinton's first educational proclamation, and 3 months after the release of Windows 95 and its accompanying Internet Explorer browser software, Gates began giving public lectures on the importance of the internet as an indispensable learning tool and the on role the internet would play in the future of American schooling. His first speech, which he addressed to more than 700 national education leaders and students at Georgetown University, was an organized public spectacle. "The most important use for information technology is to improve education," Gates told his large audience. "We have a tremendous opportunity to enhance the ways we think and learn by taking advantage of technology" (Microsoft, 1995). Reinforcing his ideas with video clips of students using the internet in classrooms, Gates introduced his concept of a "Connected Learning Community."

In this vision, students are connected between schools, between school and home, and between school and the outside world. Internet-connected classrooms offer a stimulating, enriched learning environment in which students have access to the world's information; collaborate and problem-solve with peers, teachers, and subject matter experts; and are all beautifully accommodated in terms of their individual learning styles. Teachers are coaches and facilitators in the internet-driven classroom and are able to obtain student records, immediately assess students' learning curve, and provide appropriate feedback. In addition, parents are able to connect to teachers and school activities, so that they feel involved in their children's education. "The concept of the Connected Learning Community is an exciting vision with tremendous potential," Gates said, "but we all need to work together to do our part to help."

Microsoft, Gates announced, would gladly do its share in this massive volunteer effort to get internet-based learning in schools as quickly as possible. First, he said, Microsoft software developers were working on technologies that would help facilitate home-school connectivity and would be giving this software—the Microsoft Parent-Teacher Connection Server—to schools for free. Second, the company had begun to demonstrate an apparent interest in online educational resources. As a new partner of the nonprofit internet site Global Schoolhouse, Microsoft would help to build "compelling" content, provide innovative lesson plans, class projects, teaching tools, and resource areas, and give information on in-service training, conferences, and teaching standards. In the coming months Gates would also announce a number of other web-based services accessible through the company website:

1. Microsoft.com/education: a resource site for instructors, technology professionals, and educational administrators, with

features such as the teacher network, which facilitates online discussions between educators.

2. Microsoft.com/safekids: a site offering guidelines to young users on how to search the web "safely." ("As more children connect to the Internet at home and at school," the site read, "they must learn to be street smart—even on electronic highways.")

3. Asia.microsoft.com/education/teachertraining: one of many sites for teachers from other countries to get up to speed on web-based learning.

4. Microsoft.com/encarta: the company's for-purchase, hyperlinked encyclopedia that contains audio, video, and picture resources.

In 1996, according to Schlender (1996), Microsoft was spending $400 million a year to become an internet content provider (p. 46). Joining Microsoft's sudden commitment to online learning were a number of other computer and telecommunications corporations who also began investing in internet material for schools, internet access initiatives, and school website competitions. AT&T launched the AT&T Learning Network, committing a much-touted $150 million "to help connect schools, libraries, and communities to the Information Superhighway" (Welcome, 1997). Apple's Global Education Network, Sun Microsystem's SchoolCruiser, and Disney's Edu-station were other examples of corporate America's investment in internet education.

Besides describing Microsoft's many internet educational sites, Gates announced that he would donate the proceeds from his book, *The Road Ahead* (1995), toward the technology programs that existed in 22 school districts as identified by the National Foundation for the Improvement of Education (a subsidiary of the National Educational Association). In a sense, Gates's heavily promoted speaking events also acted as a book tour. *The Road Ahead* documents Gates's personal vision of the internet as a communication, spatial navigation, business, shopping, and learning tool. His chapter on education, called "Education: The Best Investment," appears toward the end of the book, between the chapters "Friction-Free Capitalism" and "Plugged in at Home." Gates's education chapter outlined themes similar to those found in his speeches: Students will be exposed to a seemingly limitless world of information, will learn at their own pace, and will investigate questions with the help of a larger electronic community. *The Road Ahead* explains how, through technology that allows the computer to "know" the user, education will become customized according to students' individual needs:

> Many educational software programs will have distinct personalities, and the student and the computer will get to know each other. A student will ask, perhaps orally, "What caused the American Civil War?" His or her computer will reply, describing the conflicting contentions: that it was primarily a battle over economics or human rights. The length and approach of the answer will vary depending on the student and the circumstances. A student will be able to interrupt at any time to ask the computer for more or less detail or to request a different approach altogether. The computer will know what information the student has read or watched and will point out connections or correlations and offer appropriate links. If the computer knows the student likes historical fiction, war stories, folk music, or sports, it may try to use that knowledge to present the information. But this will be only an attention-getting device. The machine, like a good human teacher, won't give in to a child who has lopsided interests. Instead it will use the child's predilections to teach a broader curriculum. (p. 195)

For Gates, learning takes place as much in the classroom as it does online, with students exploring (or being explored by) customized Net spaces. Echoing the protechnology rhetoric of decades earlier, Gates painted a vision of computers replacing human beings in the classroom. According to Gates, it's not teachers, but the computers themselves (and the research and marketing teams behind these online learning experiences) that will know students' learning interests and proclivities. His protechnology, proeducation arguments had wide appeal. *The Road Ahead* became a national best-seller during the 1995 holiday season (it was released in November in anticipation of holiday sales) and was rereleased as a paperback in 1997.

CELEBRATING INTERNET EDUCATION IN TELEVISION ADS

Beginning in 1995, corporate America's sudden celebration of internet education was also visualized on television. The high-profile advertisements, broadcast during prime time, painted glorious pictures of internet learning and illustrated the important role the internet would play in young people's school and home lives. Not surprisingly, Microsoft began the ad blitz with a $100 million advertising campaign, shown between 1995 and 1997, that featured the potentially miraculous educational content the internet would bring to schools (Burstein & Kline, 1995). Each asking, "Where do you want to go today?" the ads showed viewers an idealized internet-surfing experience filled with wholesome, affirming educational and democratic conventions. One commercial, which advertised Microsoft's internet-related software, took a "user's" point of view that was fixed to the computer screen. Set to "What a Wonderful World" sung by a soft, soothing female voice, the ad began with a text screen that read, "Microsoft software helps you learn." The mouse arrow then clicked on image after image of visually appealing, value-loaded, "educational" web content: German protests at the Berlin Wall; the Berlin Wall being dismantled (at this point the audio of Martin Luther King Jr.'s "I Have a Dream" speech overtakes the music: "I have a dream my poor little children shall not be judged by the color of their skin but by the content of their character"); various planets accompanied by audio from man's first moon walk; diagrams of a heart; a photo of Mao; video of King giving a speech; a King photo with accompanying text; an image of Anne Frank; and Picasso's painting *The White Dove*, which slowly dissolves to a film image of a white dove flapping upward, presumably indicating world peace. At one point the arrow moves to a computer-menu category list and considers the selection: mathematics, physics, chemistry, earth science, paleontology, and astronomy. The arrow chooses—not surprisingly—astronomy, predictably linking technology to space exploration/enlightenment, a common theme in these commercials.

Evoking history, medicine, astronomy, and peace, the ads' depiction of internet use showed a constantly moving stream of digital images. They multiplied, changed size, or appeared as video, suggesting an experience of constant interactivity. As the ad implied, a student visiting all these websites could learn about serious and evocative world events and, more important, the nature of American democracy—in color, up close and in depth. Indeed, this was internet surfing in idealized form: The ad smartly avoided depictions of load-up times, banner advertisements, and emerging game and shopping opportunities. Beginning with this 1995 Microsoft campaign, televised images of the internet underwent a clear shift, from evoking a mysterious place that only unlikely people knew about (e.g., in a commercial showing a little-girl sage from MCI, or an IBM ad featuring internet-enlightened nuns) and a savvy means for business efficiency, to an enchanting learning paradise and celebration of internet educational content.

More education-related advertising persisted throughout 1996. As television ads laid claim to creating the best educational environment ever with the internet, they also framed the Net as the solution to a multitude of parental concerns. The focus of home use was not only education, but also the surreptitious monitoring and surveillance of adolescent behavior—or the elimination of the need for such direct parental supervision. At home with the internet, children were placed in front of their "home learning centers," oohing and ahhing as their curiosity transported them to higher levels of cognition. One 1996 advertisement for WebTV Network Inc. (acquired by Microsoft in 1997) showed three young boys positioned attentively in front of a huge living-room monitor that emitted a blue halo of light. Thus, WebTV transformed after-school sloth in front of the boob tube into an intense parlay with technology, where the medium conveniently imparted knowledge and parents could leave their children in the protective custody of a wholesome, surrogate school.

The message these ads gave to parents (and teachers) was that they need not be present to provide inspiration to children working on homework. As illustrated by a 1996 Intel commercial, all school assignments were depicted as creating positive self-directed experiences when they were done with the aid of an Intel computer chip. The commercial portrayed an elementary-aged girl researching, via the internet, a book report on jazz music. She was shown to "interact" so completely with the audio and video files supported by the computer chip that she was transported into the glowing circuitry of the chip, while expertly playing a jazz riff on a saxophone. To adequately portray children as both enchanted by and adeptly handling computers, many of these ads often highlighted the internet's interactive nature by focusing on students' hands as they clicked on the mouse or typed astute questions. Shots of the screen (constantly being modified by the mouse arrow or typed words) as extensions of the students' curiosity would follow, as well as frequent close-ups of student faces as they oohed, ahhed, and absorbed the magnitude of their choices.

If the internet could work as an educational babysitter for innocent youth, it could also function as an electronic monitor and chaper-
one for curious teenagers with rising hormone levels. In two slick
advertisements, AT&T WorldNet Service suggested ways to forever
alter teenage dating and flirting while simultaneously gaining valuable multimedia skills. The first commercial opens with a girl exiting
a car and saying good night to her date as her wary father steals a
glance from a second-floor window. Inside the house, the girl says
good night to her father and goes to her room. From the isolation of
her bedroom, however, the date resumes past reasonable hours, com-
pliments of AT&T WorldNet Service. To the tune of Patsy Cline's 1957
hit "Walkin' After Midnight," the creative and interactive capacities of
the two high school sweethearts are unleashed as they use advanced
multimedia software, computers, cameras, and scanners to cut and
paste digital love messages and send them back and forth from their
home computers.

While portraying multimedia skills as valuable, these ads also
described the social development of teens via technology in very positive ways and showed a seamless line of technology between school
and home. In another AT&T ad, which debuted during the January
1998 Super Bowl (home of U.S. television's most expensive airtime),
gossip about a teenage girl with a crush is transmitted to seemingly
everyone with the help of AT&T. Angela, the girl, entrusts her school
friends with knowledge of her fondness for Bobby Templeton. Soon,
the whole school, and then the whole world, is abuzz with the news.
The gossip doesn't travel through secret paper notes or whispered
conversations, but through computer labs, a boy at home with a computer, laser-printed love signs, cell phones, pagers, and satellites.
When Angela gets home, her mother says, "Hey Ange, that Bobby
Templeton's pretty cute." The girl replies, "You know too?!" and then
finds the real Bobby in the next room. The ad ends with a voiceover:
"Spread the word on the world's most powerful network." Besides
making kids smarter, these ads suggested, internet technology would
make teens more socially integrated and popular (a classic middle-
class concern), but they would also remain under the watchful eye of
their parents (another classic parental concern).

MCI joined Microsoft, Intel, and AT&T in 1997 as promoters of
internet education with their "Is This a Great Time, or What?" campaign. One ad in this campaign featured the notion of real-world

experts and intense internet interactivity. Starting with warm, lush, classical music and opening on a long shot of an astronaut floating happily in a space capsule, the first ad dramatized a classroom's "exciting" communication with an online expert. The expert in this commercial was a Russian astronaut—indicating a new era of Russian-American space collaboration, and gently reminding target-audience baby boomers of the Sputnik challenge and of NASA's technological achievements:

> *Russian astronaut*: Hello America!
> (A tracking shot sweeps by a row of computer-engrossed European American fourth graders in an airy, sunny classroom. The students are looking at their monitors while interacting with one another. One kid points to the screen.)
> "Ask him what's it like floating in space."
> "What?"
> (A low chatter with words like *cool* runs throughout the ad. A child's hands—in close-up—type quickly. The astronaut slowly reaches out and grabs a floating camera. We hear more questions from the entranced students.)
> "Do you ever get a chance to sleep?"
> (The shot cuts to a close-up of a cursor arrow clicking "send" on the computer screen. Text below the cursor reads, "To: Mission Control (Internet).")
> *Lauren Bacall-like voice-over*: It used to be that we just launched rockets into space.
> (A European American girl looking at the screen appears transfixed. The astronaut punches a message into his computer. Then a student's shoelace floats upward, followed by an African American girl's pigtails, a European American boy's frog [coming out of a desk], and an Asian American boy's pencil. The children appear captivated and amazed. Meanwhile we hear snippets of the kids' bursting curiosity.)
> "What's the scariest moment . . . what about coming home when the fuel's all gone?"
> *Lauren Bacall-like voice-over*: Today, through distance learning, MCI can launch entire schools.

> The lush music incorporates a plinky, happy xylophone.
> Kids—along with a globe, a book, a trumpet, and a
> lunchbox—float happily above their desks. A European
> American boy (still seated) pokes at transparent blobs
> floating out of a bottle. Finally, a black screen with white
> text (ending with an email smiley face) reads, Is this a
> great time, or what? :) MCI.

Another ad within this campaign focused on the democratic/educational potential of the web. In a rush of elegantly visualized people, symbolic school settings and stylized talking heads, the ad featured uncommonly articulate White children and an upper-class African American businessman who talk about the web as a means for equal interaction and unfettered social accessibility. Various voices narrate the copy, often overlapping to create a sort of echo effect:

> People can communicate mind to mind. Not Black to White.
> There are no genders. Not man to woman. There is no age.
> Not young and old. There are no infirmities. Not short to tall.
> Or handsome to homely. Just thought to thought. Idea to
> idea. Uninfluenced by the rest of it. There are only minds.
> Only minds . . . What is this place. Utopia? No. No. The
> Internet. It's a nice place, this place called the Internet. Is this
> a great time or what? :)

In addition to the elegant people (shot, no less, in slow motion), key words flash by quickly on computer screens (as if being typed) and on green chalkboards (where children decisively cross them out): "there is no . . . race"; "no genders"; "no age"; "there are no infirmities"; "only minds"; "utopia." Children, who were often delivering segments of the voiceover or visually crossing out words, were positioned in schools, by chalkboards and alone in library corridors. If *everyone* was on the internet, these ads suggested, we would be able to realize a wonderful world of peace, prosperity, and equality. The web, as an educative and social tool, became retooled as a social panacea.

These twin themes—education and democratic social consciousness via internet access—took off in other televised advertising campaigns. Two ads by Oracle, a computer company featuring less expensive network computers that carry little software but require an internet connection, responded to urban-suburban inequality in America and to First World–Third World inequality on a global scale. The first ad, scheduled during high-profile programs such as the 1997 World Series, was a tale of two cities and two boys. The first boy lives in an airy, picturesque suburban home with a large porch and flowering trees. The second boy lives in a dingy brick urban high-rise apartment in a neighborhood of traffic noise. The male voice-over says, "There's no question that computers open up entirely new worlds. But [cut to shots of second boy] what about children who can't afford personal computers? Fortunately, as of today, we'll never have to ask that question again" [cut to text: "Introducing Network Computers. Starting at $299."]. By this point, the two boys are smiling as they click away on their keyboards and communicate as animated dots in a chat room. The narrator concludes, "Networked computers allow everyone to join the information age, and we'd like to say welcome."

The second Oracle ad, which made an auspicious debut during the 1998 Super Bowl, purported to change the world with a new kind of "educational" revolution. The 30-second (there was also a 1-minute version) ad is laden with images of Southeast Asia, particularly of Cambodia and young people with the identifying scarves of the Khmer Rouge revolutionaries. Other "revolutionary" images, such as Soviet-style troops and leaders, are thrown in for added effect. The male voice-over says, "This revolution will be about knowledge and access [cut to shot of a young Black male in a stocking cap on a graffiti-sprayed urban basketball court], about progress and opportunity." The narrator later asks, "Where do we come in? We make the software that manages information, that will enable anyone, anywhere, to sit at the seat of knowledge." The final shot cuts from an ancient Cambodian temple to a red wooden school chair on a platform, streaked with golden light. The selection of the Khmer Rouge as the featured revolutionaries for this ad was strategic, since the Khmer Rouge had so many child soldiers who, in this revolution, could be more productively typing away on networked computers. The old-fashioned red classroom chair was also an important image to bridge the cozy one-room school house with a high-tech learning environment. Once again, internet education, according to this ad, was poised to save the world.

WHY THE CORPORATE
INTEREST IN INTERNET EDUCATION?

The many televised education-oriented internet commercials that bombarded the public between 1995 and 1998 had all aspects of the internet covered: internet-ready computers (Oracle), internet processing chips (Intel), internet software (Microsoft, Oracle) and internet access (MCI, AT&T). Other ads with similar educational and socially progressive themes (most often developed by the same computer and telecommunication companies) appeared in magazines and newspapers. The overall message was the same: If children have access to computers they will learn more, be happier, and help the world become a better place.

Even though there can be much to say about the internet's true educational potential, McChesney (1997) is quick to point out that "markets are ill-equipped to address social values except to exploit them, often perversely, in advertising messages to sell commodities" (p. 47). Education, one of the most noble causes, and one that can almost immediately engage the families of America (a broad constituency), was a theme that certainly could be exploited. While these themes could make people rally around—and share the cost in—community efforts to wire the schools, they could also make people see the benefits of a home connection and see value in Microsoft's philanthropic-sounding Connected Learning Community—links between home and school. For the American middle class, who in Garrison Keillor's words, want all their children to be "above average" and who depend upon education to get ahead (Ehrenreich, 1989), an idea like a school-home internet connection can make a powerful impression as a way to give kids an edge, and a way to get parents involved in the process. Furthermore, images of children using computers (for the most part, ads portrayed children between 8 and 11 years old) indicate an adultlike savvy on the children's part, especially since they were shown to be doing things beyond the skills of most adults. While the images pointed to a rosy, technologically satisfying future for children with the right kind of multimedia skills, they also signaled rapid antiquity for any adult not on the internet bandwagon.

With education and educational content playing such a starring role in much of the public discourse surrounding internet use between 1995 and 1998, however, internet content was only alluded to in vague and utopian terms. It was a conversation with an astronaut floating in space, or a seamless stream of planets and historical figures. These were accessible, idealistic images with no strings attached. Nothing remotely looking like advertising existed in these images. As Sussman (1997) writes, "Much of the excited rhetoric about the glorious future of the information society does not take into consideration the material and personal interests of the private institutions and governments that actually dominate it. Instead, communication technology is usually portrayed as if it's all there for anyone's taking" (p. x).

What was actually happening to web content within this same period was a different story. According to Lawrence and Giles (1999), sites that had anything to do with education were becoming drastically overshadowed by sites that pushed e-commerce. In 1997, President Clinton left his educational agenda to Vice President Al Gore (who continued to participate in NetDays, introduce educational initiatives such as the Technology Literacy Challenge Fund, and speak about "connecting children to the future") and began to push e-commerce. As Sussman (1997) has observed, "The Clinton Administration, despite its public relations efforts on behalf of an 'information superhighway,' would not venture into regulatory turf so as not to offend 'government downsizing' conservatives" (p. 182). During an address in July 1997 (only 5 months after, in his State of the Union address, he pledged education as that year's single most important priority), Clinton announced his Electronic Commerce Initiative:

> But as has already been said, one of the most revolutionary uses of the Internet is in the world of commerce. Already we can buy books and clothing, obtain business advice, purchase everything from garden tools to hot sauce to high-tech communications equipment over the Internet. But we know it is just the beginning. Trade on the Internet is doubling or tripling every single year. In just a few years, it will generate hundreds of billions of dollars in goods and services.
>
> If we establish an environment in which electronic commerce can grow and flourish, then every computer will be a window open to every business, large and small, everywhere in the world. Not only will industry leaders such as IBM be able to tap into new markets, but the smallest start-up company will have an unlimited network of sales and distribution at its fingertips. (Clinton, 1997a)

Within that same year, 1997, internet shopping activity doubled, according to a CommerceNet/Nielsen Media Research survey

(CommerceNet, 1997). The success of Amazon.com was representative of this shift. Electronic shopping opportunities had been heralded since the early 1990s in the press as a novelty: ordering a pizza online, or buying a car without experiencing the pressure from a car salesman. Amazon.com, however, turned novelty into mass consumerism by becoming the primary internet e-tailer between 1995 and 1997. Benefiting from an enormous amount of free press publicity, Amazon.com became the first internet superstore, eventually offering everything from CDs to drug prescriptions. Its overwhelming success and memorable trade name pointed to the internet's one-stop online shopping opportunities of the future.

The web's interactivity, it turned out, offered unique advantages when it came to advertising and marketing. People could easily process their own invoices (supplying names, addresses, credit card numbers, and purchase requests online) without having to go through a customer service representative. Online questionnaires and contests could help companies inexpensively figure out how to make their products and services more effective and popular (Zoll, 2000). Additionally, cookies—small electronic files that automatically fix onto users' computers each time a website is accessed—could identify the computer (and as such, the user) by transmitting back a code to the originating website and processing it in the website's databank. Cookie codes enable the website to develop purchasing profiles on web users and then eventually advertise certain products according to users' individual interests and searching tendencies. Critics have likened what occurs with cookies to the experience of being followed in a department store by someone with a legal pad, who writes down each product a shopper looks at, picks up, and purchases.

Even as cookies caused alarm in privacy groups, online companies framed cookies as a benefit to both the online business world and online shoppers. "What the better-targeted, more personalized ad will do is see that more people get ads that really mean something," said Daniel Jaffe of the National Association of Advertisers (Penkava, 1999). "This means a more competitive marketplace, a more efficient marketplace and lower cost" (p. 2). Indeed, IBM produced a television commercial in 1999 that featured internet users (played by actors) who *wanted* to be profiled and targeted. Promoting IBM's profiling software, E-business Solutions, the commercial showed a focus group of eight people sitting around a table discussing their advertising needs, while researchers observed from behind mirrored glass:

African American Man: They don't know me. I get these cata-
    logs for kids' clothes and I don't have any kids.
European American Woman #1: I get discounts for car repair. I
    take the subway.
European American Woman #2: I get offers for aluminum sid-
    ing . . . I live in an apartment.
African American Man: Hey, hey, you behind the glass! You're
    the ones with the computers and databases. You don't
    know me, you don't know them . . . you oughta know
    who we are!
Music from the song "Getting to Know You," from *The King
    and I*, plays underneath the following text: "Know what
    your customers want. IBM Business Intelligence. E-busi-
    ness Solutions. IBM: Solutions for a small planet."
African American Man (peering through glass): Hey, I think
    they got sandwiches in there . . .

Profiling, according to this scenario, is helpful for consumers
because it eliminates bothersome advertising appeals. In other
words, targeted advertising is welcome advertising. That this focus
group was conscious of the people observing them behind mirrored
glass and were comfortable (even happy) having their conversation
monitored, further suggested that cookies are a benign surveillance
mechanism, a technology with only the best interests of ordinary
people at heart.

Interestingly, because all commercial browser software, such as
Netscape or Microsoft Explorer, is automatically formatted to accept
all cookies by default, users don't tend to be aware that they are being
profiled as they search the web (Bruno & Gerrity, 2000). Furthermore,
some webpages developed ways to block user access *unless* they
accepted a cookie, making it necessary for a user to provide data in
exchange for entering a website. Cookies don't identify the names of
users and so appear innocuous. But combined with the names,
addresses, phone numbers, and other personal information that online
users/shoppers routinely give out when filling out website forms and
questionnaires, as well as a record of online purchases from a specific
website, cookies provide websites with deep profiles on individual
users. Such profiling ensures that a larger percentage of interested
shoppers respond to online ads in a positive way, allowing online

businesses to charge advertisers more money for placing ads on their websites. User-profile information can also be processed in "third party" advertising data banks and sold to other companies interested in marketing to a specific category of online user. Moreover, new developments in spyware technology (e.g., RealAudio, KaZAa)—software that users unwittingly download along with other software—allow for even better tracking of user web surfing and preferences. Spyware routinely hijacks browser homepages, sending user data directly back to advertiser and marketing data banks, not just to individual websites. Companies clearly recognized the huge marketing potential of such information-packed data banks, already significant from catalog and direct-mail data collection (Tedeschi, 2000).

With such advantages as user-profiling technologies, between 1995 and 2000, more companies rushed to market products and services on the web, stake out particular internet territories, and create an online presence. By the late 1990s, much of the information superhighway had become a vast new market for consumer goods and services, a public relations tool for consumer information and outreach, and a means for sharing consumer data between businesses.

With this in mind, it seems clear that getting people on the web between 1995 and 1998—as many people as possible—was a crucial factor in making this newly privatized, commercially based medium work as a profitable marketplace. Without admitting education's role in this agenda, Gates said as much in *The Road Ahead*. From his (and other corporate executives') perspective in 1995:

> In the rush to build the information highway, no one has seen any gold yet, and there's a lot of investing to be done before anyone does. The investments will be driven by faith that the market will be large. Neither the full highway nor the market will exist until a broadband network has been brought to most homes and businesses. Before that can happen, the software platforms, applications, networks, servers, and information appliances that will make up the highway all have to be built and deployed. Many pieces of the highway won't be profitable until there are tens of millions of users. (p. 228)

Hooking up schools (and hyping educational opportunities in the process), it seems, was part of a large-scale strategy to get America wired as quickly as possible in order for the shopping and commercialized services to begin. By 2001, nearly 100% of U.S. schools were online.

CHAPTER 3

Commercial Internet
Strategies Make Inroads in Schools

I remember watching my grandfather look overhead in awe at an air-
plane flying by. That's the way I feel about the Internet. I'm kind of in
awe over the whole thing. It's just amazing.

—High school educator, 1995

This is the first time in the history of the human race that a generation of kids has overtaken their parents in the use of new technology. Consider . . . what it means to us as marketers.

—Peter Elo, president of Lego Systems, 1999

Wiring schools to the information superhighway was the motivating
narrative for using billions in public monies for the construction of the
internet as a commercial highway in the United States. But school-age
students weren't only the cover story for the internet—they were commercial targets as well. According to the optimistic reports of industry
analysts, schools would deliver legions of young consumers to for-
profit sites.

The youth market had become increasingly valuable and lucrative
throughout the 1990s. The oft-quoted child-market analyst James
McNeal (1992) noted that "today's kid is an increasingly self-reliant
youngster, pretty savvy as a consumer, with money of his or her own
to spend, materialistic, willing to sub for the parents as a shopper,
soon to be master of the marketplace." He added that a young person
was, "in boxing terms, a lightweight with an economic power punch
whom we might nickname Kid Kustomer" (p. 3). Indeed, teenage
spending exploded throughout the 1990s, while advertising and mar-

keting efforts to reach this demographic reached new heights: $100 million in 1990 and $2 billion in 2000 (Alexander & Dichter, 2000). Marketing predictions also signaled that this materialistic population of 12-to-19-year-old "Kid Kustomers" in the United States would expand, from 29.1 million in 2000 to 34.9 million in 2010 (Zollo, 1995).

Not surprisingly, many corporations simply assumed that the spend-happy kid customers would want to spend their money online. A study by the media research firm Jupiter Communications indicated just how lucrative this group would be, if targeted via the internet: Online shopping by teenagers 13–18 years old reportedly totaled $300 million by the end of 2000 and seemed to be accelerating twice as fast as the rate of adults who shopped online. The study predicted that by 2003, teenagers would be spending $2 billion annually on internet-based merchandise (Siegal, 2000). A subsequent study by the same firm predicted that kids and teens would spend more than double the amount—$4.9 billion—via the internet by 2005 and would make $21.4 billion worth of purchases in bricks-and-mortar stores on the basis of information they found on the internet (Jupiter, 2000).

A bounty of new market-analysis studies also discovered that children helped their parents shop online, took charge of pointing and clicking 48% of the time, and suggested websites to buy from 42% of the time (NFO, 2001). Other online developments, such as internet shopping cards, facilitated teen purchasing power. DoughNet, iCanBuy, Cobaltcard, PocketCard, and E-wallet emerged, for example, to help young people shop, bank, and even donate to charities online through special prepaid accounts, or by drawing directly from a teen's bank account (Pugh, 2000).

It also seemed that members of the youngest generation of online users were not bothered by advertising. In fact, they came to expect it on websites and were comfortable sharing personal information in order to win prizes or be able to play a particular game (e.g., Clausing, 1999). One study released in 2000 reported that if a prize was involved, two thirds of children ages 10–17 would provide commercial website operators with the names of their favorite stores, and more than half would give their parents' favorites (Associated, 2000). Along with showing their responsiveness to online promotions, young users were developing "multitasking" skills, which allowed them to digest corporate advertising as they worked on some other internet-based (or other) activity

(Walters, 1999). As a communications medium, the internet had possibly more marketing potential than had any mass medium before it.

Moreover, it seemed like schools were a potential goldmine to internet marketers. Schools were wired, and there were no effective restrictions on internet advertising and marketing practices geared toward children. Congress had passed the Children's Online Privacy Protection Act (COPPA) in 1998 to better protect children's online privacy, but it didn't amount to much. The act, which would become effective in April 2000, concerned only those websites trying to collect online information from children 13 and under. Besides mandating that these commercial websites post prominent notices detailing the kind of information gathered, how it would be used, and whether it would be shared, the COPPA required that the sites obtain verifiable consent from parents and enable parents to delete all information collected if they wanted to. Three months after COPPA went into effect, however, the Federal Trade Commission (FTC) found that few companies were complying with the regulations. "Of the sites that did collect kids' personally identifiable information," the FTC reported, "roughly half appeared to have substantial compliance problems" ("Web Sites," 2000). What's more, only 16% of children under age 13— the age group affected by COPPA—were inclined to give out personal information on the web. The more significant group of information sharers—39% of children ages 13 to 17 (and a far more valuable consumer market)—would never be affected by COPPA. Furthermore, the public's attitude toward commercialized content in classrooms, as noted in Chapter 1, had softened incredibly by the 1990s. Plenty of teachers today see internet advertising as hardly disruptive or invasive. Online ads are not a problem, since advertising messages are "everywhere" already.

A Canadian marketing publication called *Strategy* captured the industry's excitement at potentially reaching a young audience during the daytime hours. Canada had actually beaten the United States in school connectivity and was in fact "leading the world in wired schools." *Strategy* described the implications this would have for commerce:

> Within the school system, young Canadians are being encouraged to use the Internet for research and information gathering. And they seem to be listening. Among teens, the most common reason for using the Net—aside from socializing via instant messaging and email—is to do homework. . . . The implication for all this for mar-

keters is pretty clear: Canadians are integrating the Internet into their lives at an early age. And where they are, so should marketers be. (Thoburn, 2000, p. 23)

Carole Walters, who works as a media director in the advertising industry and serves on the American Association of Advertising Agencies Interactive Marketing and New Media Committee, noted in 1999 that providing educational content in schools while promoting other services created a favorable situation for both schools and corporations. Writing to her fellow advertising colleagues, Walters raved about the internet's exciting educational possibilities (e.g., virtually visiting different places, designing itineraries, getting to know Shakespeare, and corresponding with peers). Then she added, "By dedicating some of our effort to this, we will help ourselves in the long run. We will have aided in the development of a population of future employees whose creativity has been nurtured, not squelched. Consider an environment where individuals can think through, and understand, everything from transactional spreadsheets to an advertising concept!" (p. 283). Not surprisingly, corporations leapt at the opportunity to market to America's youth via the internet. "When added to the psychological and sociological studies that advertisers are investing in to find out what motivates kids on-line," Zoll (2000) wrote, "we can safely say that on-line commercial marketing to children has become a formidable force" (p. 1).

STICKY PORTALS AND BANNER ADS

Beginning in 1995, the business sector was increasingly abuzz with marketing reports describing the internet's revolutionary advertising potential, especially with internet portals. A portal, unlike a webpage, is an entry point to a collection of many decentralized online resources. The internet's commercial future, according to industry analysts, was in the "stickiness" of content portals and in the precision of banner ads, which began appearing at the top of webpages in 1996. If users stayed "stuck" on a certain page long enough, then they would have a chance to read, digest, and respond to the commercial messages, which would be precisely targeted to their interests. Commercial websites aimed for stickiness. A site selling clothing and jewelry to teenagers, like delias.com, for example, tried to create a cultural context that included chat rooms, original magazine-style content, and relevant information alongside their purchase selections in order to attract young consumers to their Net space. "On Web sites selling to teenagers, the merchandise often seems like an afterthought" Siegal (2000) wrote. "First you have to set the mood with music, offer gossipy tidbits about rock stars and actors (just how long will Leo's [the actor, Leo DeCaprio's] affair with a model last?) and provide advice, chat room and concert information. Then you can sell clothing" (p. 1). Money and energy went into portal development. Key portals like Yahoo! and AOL enhanced their offerings so that users never really had to leave the portal page; they encouraged users to personalize their web spaces (e.g., MyYahoo!, MyAOL), to increase their reliance on the commercial portal (and its advertising); they practiced "framing," linking to other pages without ever revealing the original URL of the linked page; and "mousetrapping"—disabling the Back button on a user's browser so users are unwillingly locked, or mousetrapped, into the site. The strategy, long used by the pornography and gambling industries, became a typical tactic for mainstream sites.

So as to better target the advertising (ad relevance added to a portal's stickiness), companies also began compiling and sharing personal information about internet users. The advertising firm Doubleclick became especially good at gathering user data, collected through cookies and surveys for direct-marketing purposes. Although website cookies don't reveal a user's name and address, they do establish where a user is accessing from, his or her country and type of establishment, and the websites he or she is accessing. Doubleclick used this information against its growing database of banner advertisements, and matched advertisers to the web user's profile. "While we don't know who exactly you are," Doubleclick's president said in 1999, "there are about 20 to 25 things we can tell about an individual" ("Stakes," 1999). Consequently, any kind of information to better target a user became desirable. Many websites began to sell their customer information to companies like Doubleclick—names, addresses, and product preferences that they had gathered through product purchases through their site. Doubleclick would cross-reference this data with other user-access data and deliver personal profiles on web users that were both accurate and constantly evolving along with their tastes and interests. The strategies appeared to be working. Online sales began to climb, going from a modest $3 billion in 1997 to $33 billion in 1999. Industry analysts predicted that online spending that resulted from banner ads would reach $199 billion in 2005.

Consequently, providing sticky educational portals to students, complete with highly targeted advertising, became a significant marketing strategy for targeting young people in and out of school. By the late 1990s, companies had rolled out a number of competing commercial educational portals—ZapMe!, HomeworkCentral, Yahooligans!, Lightspan, Britannica.com, BigChalk, HiFusion, Imind, MindSurf, SchoolCity, Blue Web'N, Eduhound, and Education Planet—that all fused educational content (mostly aggregated links to other known sites) with in-your-face advertising and shopping opportunities. Much was made about the many educational links on these sites, which were categorized under broad subject headings (Literature, History, Science, etc.) and selected by "highly qualified content experts." To make their services even more indispensable, the portals added email, reference, career guide, and webpage personalization services to their offerings. The hope was that students would find these services so helpful for their schoolwork and communication needs that they would extend their portal usage to after-school hours, where their parents could access the portal as well.

ZapMe! was especially flagrant in its attempt to both educate and market to students during school. In an arrangement similar to that used by Channel One, ZapMe! "gave" entire computer labs to schools with the agreement that students had to be logged onto the ZapMe! Net space for 4 hours every school day. ZapMe! schools also had to hand over students' personal data so the company could better target its commercial elements to individual students. The company positioned banner ads on both the top and bottom of its interface and placed a "dynamic billboard" (a constantly moving, interactive ad) on the bottom left of the screen. Every activity a student performed on the lab's computer was framed by these advertisements, even word processing. The company gained particular notoriety for its ZapPoints, ZapCash, and ZapMall programs (Fabos, 2000, Parija, 1999). Students earned points every moment they surfed the web, and they could redeem their points "for all sorts of cool stuff" at the ZapMall. ZapMe!'s ZapCash program was a way for students to interact directly with their bank accounts. By the fall of 1999, 2000 schools had signed up for the ZapMe! deal, and 15,000 were on the waiting list, mostly because of the free computers. ZapMe!'s stock was worth half a billion dollars and the company hoped to reach a student audience of 10 million by 2002—which was 2 million more than Channel One (Schwartz, 2000).

THE MARKETING IS THE MESSAGE

Given the increasingly overwhelming amount of data available on the web, commercial educational portals, which ostensibly grouped the most academically useful websites by subject, seemed like a good idea. The problem with these portals, however, was that more efforts were clearly placed behind the marketing and shopping elements than on the educational content. It was painfully obvious, for example, that most of ZapMe!'s resources were geared toward marketing schemes, and little thought or effort seemed to be given to the 13,000 educational links provided in ZapMe!'s main directory, which was marketed as an end-all resource for students. For example, a student would have trouble trying to find a link to the most prominent African American organization in the United States, the NAACP, under the "African American Culture" category. Although ZapMe! content editors provided prominent links to "The BlackMarket.com" (offering products, services, and feature stories for the African American community) and the "Kwanzaa Information Center" (sponsored by the MelaNet Marketplace), the NAACP was noticeably absent. ZapMe! also celebrated its Newsstand section, which ostensibly linked to newspapers around the world, but didn't include papers from countries like Australia or Canada. Many of the links were also broken or inaccessible. Certainly, a good number of websites located within the ZapMe! Net space were valuable educational resources, but one could hardly call the directory an all-encompassing information tool (or in ZapMe!'s words, "a rich storehouse of information" and "the ultimate environment for getting the facts").

ZapMe!'s own corporate pages revealed where the company's priorities lay. Its management team had backgrounds in information technology systems, computer superstore chains, consumer database marketing, children's product and multimedia entertainment, and global information technology services. Noticeably missing were educators. Perhaps even more telling were ZapMe!'s employment announcement pages. As a rapidly growing company in December 1999, ZapMe! reported that it needed people to

- coordinate with copywriters and the Content group to integrate appropriate content into promotions
- work with teachers to gain priorities and make recommendations on what courses and curricula to prioritize

- promote and implement revenue-generating shopping experiences for parents of teens within the ZapMe! e-commerce site, and
- develop programs that leveraged the ZapMe! school relationship to attract parents to shop with ZapMe!

Judging from these announcements, ZapMe! wanted to expand its resources into teacher training and the development of actual courses that were highly dependent on the ZapMe! interface. The company also wanted to develop new ways for parents and teens to use the interface at home in order to integrate the ZapMe! portal (and its many e-commerce opportunities) into their home lives. These strategies were intended to push ZapMe! use well beyond the daily 4-hour in-school requirement, with the hope that ZapMe! would become an indispensable curriculum content, communication service, and shopping mall, 24 hours a day.

As it turned out, ZapMe! and most other commercial educational initiatives failed by 2001. It seemed that ZapMe! in particular, failed because of its unabashedly commercialized internet content. Beginning in January 2000, a broad coalition of advocates, headed by Gary Ruskin of the public watchdog group Commercial Alert, sent a letter to all 50 governors to bring ZapMe!'s marketing practices to public attention. The letter charged ZapMe! with taking advantage of "a captive audience of children," turning students into "guinea pigs for advertising and marketing firms," and transforming schools and teachers into "instruments of corporate marketing" ("Coalition," 2000) News of the letter reached the *New York Times*, and ZapMe! executives found themselves defending the core of their corporate strategies. Other articles soon appeared in *Newsweek, The Wall Street Journal, U.S. News and World Report, Mother Jones, The Nation, Salon.com Magazine, Education Week,* and the *School Library Journal.*

ZapMe! responded to the criticism by quietly changing their "ZapMall" link on the main page to an "Entertainment" button, getting rid of the ZapPoints and ZapCash programs, and burying other controversial elements of their interface. Despite these efforts, the bad publicity had clearly affected the company. Advertisers no longer wanted to associate their brand with ZapMe! and its stock, which had been worth $13.75 at its height, plummeted to $2. The company's founder, Lance Mortensen (formerly the CEO of the Monterey Pasta Company), gave a dumbfounded reaction to criticism that the company made commercial intrusions into students' school lives. "The privacy thing is mind-boggling because we never took a student's address, never took a student's phone number," he told the *New York Times*. "It's heartbreaking to me that the opportunity we gave America's schools was taken away by a few people" (Schwartz, 2000, pp. 1–2). As did the public relations information on the ZapMe! website, Mortensen framed the company objective as educational—a way to solve the digital divide—not as an advertising-delivery, market research, and surveillance venture.

By November 2000, ZapMe! had collapsed as an educational service and had changed its business plan to selling satellite internet services to businesses. ZapMe!'s end was a victory for both privacy and child advocates, and certainly a victory for education. At least it appeared to be. As ZapMe! was being publicly lambasted and held up as the worst example of online educational practices, other commercial educational portals were watching and learning from ZapMe!'s mistakes. Homeworkcentral removed the shopping buttons on its main interface. Other commercial education portals adjusted their corporate strategies to appease the privacy-advocacy groups and to make their services appear to have the interests of the student users as their first priority. None of these services would be touched by the same kind of public wrath that led to ZapMe!'s demise.

Still, within a year, most of these commercial education portals (indeed, many content portals in general) followed ZapMe! into oblivion. One could certainly cite mismanagement and overinflated company expectations—as in the case of Imind. The company's former employees were so angry at their CEO and his misguided excess that they developed a parody of the educational portal, complete with satiric haikus and photographs (Imind, 2003). Internet technology stocks also crashed in 2000, prompting Wall Street to demand immediate profitability for internet ventures. Another more pervasive reason for the collapse of so many educational portals—not to mention all advertising-supported websites—was that banner advertisements were just not working. The novelty had worn off, and click-through rates were rapidly decreasing. The industry responded by making banner ads more eye-catching and interactive. In February 2001, the Interactive Advertising Bureau issued standards for seven new, larger ad formats—"skyscrapers" and "large rectangles"—that would permeate the content of a webpage, following a newspaper model. Pop-up and pop-under ads also became more plentiful, requiring internet users to actively click boxes closed before accessing website material or after closing out of a browser. "Internet users should expect more ads and new ads, such as cartoons floating across the screen, transparent ads and mini-games," reported Jonathan Lambeth in the *London Daily Telegraph*. "Whatever its appearance, online advertising desperately needs to find a way to increase its 'click-through,' or success rate" (2001, p. 2). Consequently, by mid-2001, users who logged on to bigchalk.com were greeted by Toucan Sam, the familiar Kellogg's Froot Loops icon, who swooped down across the entire bigchalk interface as the page loaded up. Students were asked to "play the Toucan Sam Tree Toss Game," which ultimately steered students to the toucansam.com website and asked them to fill out a form to win a free computer. However, none of these efforts had great results. Shortly after the Toucan trial, bigchalk.com (which had already absorbed HomeworkCentral) folded.

When it came to educational portals or any commercial, youth-targeted website, it seemed that actual click-through rates were not the real problem. As the demographic most susceptible to banner advertising (Reuters, 2000), young people actually *were* clicking on banner advertisements, and with abandon. But they weren't buying anything, and the reason was because—in retrospect this is painfully obvious—they don't own credit cards. This major miscalculation by market analysts makes all the earlier postulations about teen online spending now seem preposterous. Students spent, on average, only $31 on online merchandise in 2001. As Rachel Konrad (2002) explained, teens are impulse buyers, and it's simply more convenient to head to the mall with some cash than it is to beg parents for use of their Visa. (As the long list of now-defunct shopping card companies indicates, teens were not using these either.) Today, most commercial sites, such as Amazon.com, completely ignore shoppers under the age 18. For educational portals so dependent upon students to act on their desires, this reality did not bode well for their survival.

EDUCATIONAL PORTALS
AS BRANDING OPPORTUNITIES

Not counting Britannica.com and Lightspan, which both folded their portals into larger, fee-based educational services, only two main educational portals survived the fallout of 2000 and the years beyond. One of them was AOL@School. Launched to much fanfare in 2000, the Time Warner subsidiary was quickly endorsed by governors in six states and administrators (not teachers) as "the premier learning tool for K–12 students" (AOL, 2001). By 2002, the new education portal was adopted by 36% of U.S. schools and had a presence in all 50 states (AOL, 2002). AOL@School caters to K–12 students, as well as teachers and administrators, and unlike its precursors, it carries no banner advertising. Instead, the portal is heavily sponsored by a growing list of partners. Some partners offer products (e.g., Dell, Office Depot, Peterson's), which are featured on the "School Supplies" page. Other sponsors offer content (e.g., BrainPOP, KidsEdge), which is heavily integrated into the portal's educational links. Other partners are subsidiaries of Time Warner (e.g., *Time* magazine, CNN, and Warner Bros., AOL@School's corporate parent).

Yahooligans! is the other educational portal that has managed to stay healthy. Unveiled in 1996, Yahooligans! has long established itself as a safe and educational destination for children K–8 and has been popular among teachers since its release (Paul & Williams, 1999). Unlike AOL@School, Yahooligans! carries busy banner ads, but it is quickly apparent that almost all the ads are for some aspect of Yahooligans! web offerings (its kid-friendly news service, its safe-surfing guide, its movie information). External sponsorship also exists. For example, in 2002, Yahooligans! staged a "Name the Hottest Toys!" contest. The poll asked kids to vote on what they really wanted to get for the holiday season based on a list recommended by KBtoys.com. The kids (23,000 responded) could then email their favorite toy picks to their parents or grandparents, who were linked directly to the KBtoys.com website, where they could, ostensibly, buy the toy (Yahoo!, 2002).

While sponsorship and "hot toy" gimmicks may be financially beneficial for both Yahoo! and AOL@School, neither company depends upon these strategies for survival. Both companies are enormous and highly capitalized and therefore can afford to use their educational sites as long-term initiatives to better brand their companies. As such, they depend upon establishing a friendly presence in kids' lives when the children are young, acclimating them to the corporate brand and retaining loyal customers. Both Time Warner and Yahoo! now operate internet service providers (ISPs), which connect people to the internet. They also operate competing email and IM services (MSN is another intense rival). By converting children to their educational subsidiaries at an early age, AOL and Yahoo! create a continuous flow of new users to their regular portal services. In other words, these companies do not need to meet demands for immediate profitability that plagued other educational portal start-ups; they can use their portals as conduits to their other commercial platforms; the payoff can come later.

This is not to say that AOL@School and Yahooligan!'s educational offerings are not valuable. To the contrary, the links—many of them drawn from a small pool of government and university-sponsored projects—can be extremely useful for teachers and students. But the links overall are not overwhelmingly comprehensive. For example, a 2003 AOL@School search using the term *Johnny Appleseed* yielded six links: one crossword puzzle, two craft pages, two dead links, and one link that merely listed Johnny Appleseed's real name. (The same search in 2002 yielded a PR page [targeting kids] from the Processed Apples Institute ["Welcome AJ and the Jammin' Juicers!"] as the first link. Perhaps a little too commercial, that link is now gone). Johnny Appleseed is a staple of American history, but AOL@School clearly fails with this flimsy selection of sites.

FOR BETTER OR FOR WORSE?: EDUCATION WITH COMMERCIAL SEARCH ENGINES

Despite the increasing penetration of AOL@School, and the ubiquity of Yahooligans!, educational portals are ultimately not the way students access the web. Commercial search engines, not educational portals, are the tool of choice. A study conducted by the Pew Internet and American Life Project in 2002 found that 85% of students used an online search engine to find information (Internet, 2002). A subsequent study, conducted by the same organization a year and a half later, revealed that commercial search engines have largely replaced libraries altogether as a venue for college student research. Teachers also gravitate to search engines. "Evidence shows that educators prefer search engines because the results include information from a much wider variety of sources," writes Pete MacKay (2003) in the popular educational journal *Technology and Learning.* "As one surveyed teacher replied, 'I would rather cull the search responses on Google than deal with what [a portal] thinks is appropriate for kids'" (p. 34).

Besides their having a perceived breadth, search engines are also tremendously easy to use, and gratifying. Results come automatically;

a user can feel the power of search engines and appreciate the extensiveness of the web in gleaning thousands upon thousands of hits. And there is no getting lost within the deep links of a subject directory's database. A Back button returns a user to the main search results page. In 2003, search engines continued to be the most visited locations on the web. It is this growing dependence on search engines, however, that has led to their increased commercialization, their success as a business enterprise, and their erosion as trustworthy informational tools.

Search engines were once considered a failed business idea because they were only a conduit to other pages. In other words, they lacked stickiness; no one stayed long enough to see the advertising. In response to this crisis, search engine portals tried to develop new services to attract and retain users. For example, AltaVista spent millions to develop new portal content that it hoped would make it a comprehensive web portal for not only searches but also other activities such as in news, travel, and shopping. Google resisted such efforts, and instead focused on being the best syndicated search engine provider, with the most relevant search results. However, analysts mocked Google for its seeming lack of a means to make money from its singular mission of search excellence.

Then, search engine portals began experimenting with sponsored links—a list of two or three paying sites that appear above the actual search results. Because sponsored links are so highly targeted (they directly relate to the search terms that users type in), they became enormously profitable. A small company dealing with specialized golf equipment, for example, could sponsor a link that accompanied a user's search on golf, directly targeting the golfer. Oftentimes because users didn't know the difference between sponsored and actual searches, they were clicking sponsored links 12 to 17% of the time (Waters, 2003) (far in excess of the less than 1% banner ad click-through rate today) (Harvey, 2003b). And every time a user clicked on a sponsored link, the search engine earned money. Not surprisingly, search engine services barely distinguished between the sponsored and nonsponsored categories in order to generate more click-throughs.

When understanding the search engine industry and its gradual and quiet commercialization, it is important to understand the distinctions between the three facets of the search engine industry: search engine providers, search engine portals, and commercial search engine providers.

   Search engine providers own and manage web indexes—huge data-bases of webpages. They have also developed complicated algorithms (basically a step-by-step procedure) for searching (or "crawling") their indexes quickly, comprehensively, and *impartially*. Google, for example, the most popular search engine provider, prioritizes sites according to a "link analysis" strategy: It determines a site's popularity based on the number of other sites that have links pointing to it. Because the task of developing a huge web index is so enormous, there were only five major search engine providers in 2003: Google, AlltheWeb, Inktomi, Teoma, and AltaVista, each with its own unique algorithm, which it syndicated to search engine portals.

   Search engine portals are websites powered by a search engine provider (most often one of the top five). For example, in 2003, the portals Yahoo!, Netscape, and AOL, as well as thousands of smaller websites (e.g., MarthaStewart.com) were all powered by Google. Indeed, Google made half its revenue from selling its search technology to various websites (Harvey, 2003a). The search portal Lycos was powered by AlltheWeb. MSN, Amazon.com, and eBay were powered by Inktomi. AskJeeves was powered by Teoma, and Hotbot was powered by four search engine providers—Google, AlltheWeb, Inktomi, and Teoma. These different relationships explain why some search engine services (e.g., Yahoo! and Netscape) have more similar results than others: They are powered by the same search engine provider (Google). However, to complicate the matter, a few search engine providers, such as Google, AlltheWeb, and AltaVista also operate "branded" search engine portals. Google operates the most popular search portal, processing 55% of all search engine queries in 2003 (Nunberg, 2003); AlltheWeb remains an especially popular search engine portal throughout Europe and has a growing following in the United States. AltaVista operated one of the first popular search engine portals and is only now trying to resurrect its faded glory after its earlier redesign missteps.

   If the operations of search engines weren't already complicated enough, there is a third kind of company in the mix—*commercial search providers*. These companies broker commercial sponsorships for web search results and syndicate their services to search portals. Commercial search providers, then, act a lot like search engine providers in that they syndicate their search technology—the major difference is that they search through a database of advertisers.

   Accordingly, most search engine portals ally themselves with both an impartial search engine provider and a commercial search engine provider and run the two searches side by side, with the results appearing in separate locations on the search result list. That's the way it worked, at least in the beginning. Then came Overture. Launching in 1998 as Goto.com and changing its name in 2001, Overture quickly developed a large advertiser index and successfully brokered "sponsored sites" that appeared above and beside actual search results. However, Overture's main success came from its "Pay-For-Performance" strategy. Overture basically sold advertisers priority placement *within the supposedly impartial result list itself.* The higher an advertiser's bid, the higher the website was placed in a search result list. High placement within a search result list is important for two reasons. First, users trust this list because they mistakenly believe it impartially prioritizes websites according to the key terms entered. Second, users typically don't tend to look beyond the first two or three pages in a search result list, believing that the first two pages are the most relevant (Lasica, 2001). As such, Overture stacked each search result list with the websites of paying customers, which appeared on the first, and sometimes second, page of the list. Because the idea was instantly profitable—especially compared to the earlier search engine portal strategy of banner ads—most of the major search portals on the web began to syndicate Overture's services. One Lycos executive justified the practice this way:

> We thought long and hard and decided it doesn't matter if we are paid for a link, so long as the results are what the user wants . . . the industry has trained users to avoid anything that looks commercial. By calling them paid listings, it hurts the user. (Lasica, 2001, p. 2)

Indeed, the growing justification among internet industry folk was that people generally use the web for commercial purposes anyway. They use the web to find flower delivery services, or to purchase a barbecue grill. By 2004, Overture had signed up more than 100,000 advertisers (Overture, 2003c) and was distributing its for-profit search results to tens of thousands of websites across the internet, including MSN, Yahoo!, Netscape, AOL, Infospace and ESPN.com. These websites retained their impartial search provider (e.g., Google), but cross-listed this database with Overture's growing index of sponsored web links. In a single quarter of 2002, Overture facilitated 563 million "paid introductions" and made $126 million, compared with Google's approximately $15 million in revenue for its main business of running impartial searches (Overture, 2003b).

Accordingly, searches became increasingly stacked with sponsored websites, unbeknownst to internet users. Alarmed that the supposedly objective search result lists of nearly all search engines had become front-loaded with commercial sites, the consumer activist group Commercial Alert successfully pressured the FTC to conduct a study on deceptive search engine practices. Completed in June 2002, the study reported, not surprisingly, that the web's largest search engines did not reveal the preferred treatment they accorded to sponsors. Indeed, Google was the *only* search engine that met FTC criteria in terms of disclosing money influences in the display of search results. The FTC's response was to call for self-regulation, which was another way of tacitly turning a blind eye to the pay-for-performance strategy (Associated, 2002).

In the meantime, new developments in commercial search practices made the search engine result list even more commercial heavy. AlltheWeb, Inktomi, Teoma, and AltaVista—the top search engine providers except for Google—instigated "paid inclusion" programs: Advertisers pay a search engine provider to frequently review their webpages with its search engine crawler. Basically, paid inclusion guarantees that the website gets considered for all the engine's searches. It does not guarantee the website's rank within the search results, but it does guarantee inclusion somewhere, and for niche topics, this bodes well for the advertiser. As reporter Chris Gaither (2003) explains, "Internet companies have realized that, if someone is hunting for information on a topic like mesothelioma, the person is ripe for specialized advertising" (p. F1). A key part of the flat fee also involves advice on how to write advertisers' listings so as to further enhance their position. "Since [commercial search engines] alone understand how the algorithms inside their search engine 'black boxes' work," *Financial Times* reporter Richard Waters observed, "they generally know how to game the system, though it is a power they claim to use responsibly" (Waters, 2003).

Only one search engine provider/portal has resisted both pay-for-placement and paid inclusion. Google has taken an admirable stance on search engine integrity since its inception and has refused to allow any direct commercial influence in its search result lists. This is not to say that Google's result lists are free from market influence. An entire mini-industry exists to influence placement with the databases of impartial search engines. The search engine optimization (SEO) market, which offers "positioning" and "advisory & marketing" services to its clients, continues to flourish. These small SEO companies, which try to secure prominent listings for their clients, are sharply focused on Google, a sort of Holy Grail for SEOs. In fact, one of the most typical promotional statements appearing on these companies' websites concerns the ability to crack the patterns behind Google's objective search results. "We understand the 'spidering' schedule that Google employs," says Morevisibility.com. "By submitting at the appropriate intervals, we are able to systematically deep-penetrate the Google database" ("More Visibility," 2003). Meanwhile, as Fiona Harvey of the *Financial Times* has reported, "So many small companies have sprung up in this field that Google engineers spend much of their time tweaking its search criteria in order not to fall prey to them" (2003b, p. 32). Moreover, since Google's algorithm strategy is based on the number of links pointing to a site (ostensibly making it more popular), for-profit entities have become savvy to the linking game, working with other companies to increase the number of links leading to their websites. Calling this scheme "horizontal marketing," the company LinkBrokerage.com explains that "the more sites you can get your link on, the better chance to increase traffic." EGS Brokerage also offers a "reciprocal" linking service for all health- and insurance-related websites. "Reciprocal links with websites that have a common theme increases your popularity in the search engines, boosts your rankings, and provide a service for your customers," the company's promotional material reads (EGS, 2003). As much as Google wants to be the *New York Times* of search engines, the insistent pressure from commercial forces makes this nearly impossible.

This newfound profitability of elite and above-the-fray search engine providers—through pay-for-placement and paid inclusion programs—has made them a desirable acquisition for the bigger players in the internet industry. In late 2002, Yahoo!, which had just released its own search technology (one that was loosely based on Google's idea), bought Inktomi for $235 million. "The paid-inclusion model is really icing on the cake," said Yahoo! chief financial officer Sue Decker in 2003. "That alone really justifies the price of the transaction" (Reuters, 2003). In another bold move a few months later, Overture bought both AlltheWeb ($70 million) and AltaVista ($140 million). For a company controlling both impartial search engine providers and a bank of 100,000 (and growing) advertisers, these deals enabled endless sponsorship opportunities for Overture. And with a final sweep a few months later, Yahoo! bought Overture (including AlltheWeb and AltaVista) for $1.63 billion, securing the company as the reigning emperor of the search engine industry. Meanwhile, Microsoft also got into the search engine business in 2003 by employing over 200 engineers to work solely on search technology, and by releasing its own algorithm, MSNbot, to compete directly with Google. "We want to be a leader in search," a project manager for Microsoft's MSN told a reporter in June 2003 (Francisco, 2003). Rumors also circulated that Microsoft would buy Google, while other market analysts awaited Google's long-discussed public offering. Time Warner is the only large web property that does not yet have a stake in the search engine business, which, by 2007, is expected to reach $7 billion (Elkin, 2003).

As people habitually turn to commercial search engines to navigate an overwhelming web environment, they are unaware of the increasing difficulties of locating content that is *not* commercial or indirectly influenced by commercial interests. They are unaware of the misleading motives of the internet navigation tools they use and of the constant efforts among for-profit enterprise to bend the internet toward their ends. Robert McChesney wrote in 1998 that "advertisers and commercialism arguably have more influence over internet content than anywhere else" (p. 24). Considering the above examples, he could not have been closer to the truth. The web is being colonized by commercial interests and big media companies. This, however, is certainly not surprising. Given the history of media technology, which all showed democratic potential in their developmental phases, and given the economic and political structure in which we live, which favors commercial enterprise, we can expect that the medium will be controlled and dominated by market forces. What happens, then, when such a medium is used in schools as a legitimate and presumably neutral information source? What happens when the commercial highway runs right through the classroom?

PART II

A Commercial Highway
in Every Classroom

CHAPTER 4

Educators and Librarians
Address the Commercialized Web

The more I use the Internet, particularly the World Wide Web, the more I believe we need to introduce to students an element of skepticism about anything that they find in Internet searching.
—Barbara Safford, professor of library science, 1996

It *is* my education. I get all my information off the Internet. I don't even look at books anymore.
—High school boy, Pew Internet Study, 2002

In 2002, it became evident that students did use the internet as an information superhighway. The Pew Internet and American Life Project surveyed approximately 2,000 students from middle and high schools across the United States about teen internet use. The researchers reported that 94% of 12- to 17-year-olds turn to the internet for their school research; 71% rely on the internet as their major, if only, resource (Levin & Arafeh, 2002). According to another Pew study conducted that same year, college students rarely go inside their college library. Moreover, when they do visit the library, most of their time there is spent checking email, doing instant messaging, and surfing the web rather than conducting academic research. Like middle school and high school students, college students tend to do their academic work at home, on the web, using commercial search engines, not library databases (Rainie, Kalehoff, & Hess, 2002). "Students prefer to locate information or resources via search engine above all other options, and Google is the search engine of choice," wrote Jill Griffiths and Peter Brophy about U.K. students in 2002. "Students either have little awareness of alternative ways of finding information to the search engine route or have tried other methods and still prefer to use Google—a situation we now refer to as the Googling phenomenon" (p. 6). Kapoun (1998), who works as a college librarian at Southwest State University, has similarly noted that "students seem to gravitate to the Web first and grudgingly consult paper materials after" (p. 522). They admit that the glitz on many websites can be distracting, but educators have also postulated that maybe students—having grown up with MTV and an increasingly commercialized culture—are attracted to it, have come to expect it, and as such prefer doing their research online in a multimedia environment rather than using other, more "boring" library sources (e.g., Gardner, Benham, & Newell, 1999).

While students are using search engines almost exclusively, it also seems that search engines are not serving them well. Observations of student web use made by educators and librarians have echoed these findings. They admit a sense of lost control over the quality of research data retrieved by students and are often shocked by how students do research online. Reporting that students become both overwhelmed and confused by the number of hits they typically retrieve from search engine queries, some researchers conclude that undirected, school-related web use can be a miserable waste of time. For example, Arnold and Jayne (1998) write:

> Students are often working with broad and as yet unfocused topics, trying to search the Web at a prefocus exploration state when their anxiety level is high. To make things even more difficult, they are searching in an environment where more specific inquiries and focused searching work better. Most of the time the search engines give them an overwhelming number of hits on a broad topic such as "the flat tax," typical of the topics that freshmen are often researching. (p. 47)

While Arnold and Jayne relate stories of students wandering off "into the glitter-paved, hypertext-linked pathways of the Web" (see also Claus-Smith, 1999), they further note that student anxiety is countered by the immediate gratification of typing in a keyword and getting instant feedback on the screen. Indeed, this is a second observation reported by educators and librarians—that the search engines are often detrimentally easy for students. Moreover, most students seem to trust internet resources regardless of their editorial quality. "Unfortunately," Berger (1998) states, "many students think that if they find it on the Web, then it must be true." Both Arnold and Jayne (1998) and Safford (1996) would agree with this position, and they actually attribute students' "reverential" trust of online information to media hyperbole and political enthusiasm about the promise of inter- net resources as an educational panacea and "information highway." "The President [Clinton] calls it that, the media call it that, and we call it that," Safford wrote in 1996, right in the midst of the Education Challenge campaign. "Information means facts to most people. Therefore what we read on the Information Highway must be fact. We must dissuade students of this myth" (p. 43). Studies have confirmed some of these observations, reporting that most students trust the information they gather from search engines. In a survey of 1,693 mid- dle school students, Susan Gibson and Joanne Tranter (2000) found that 62.5% of their participants felt that 50–70% of the information they found online was true, and 21.8% felt that 80–100% was true. "Lots of studies have shown us that kids need to be reminded con- stantly to verify the source of the information they use in homework assignments and research papers," writes Walter Minkel of the *School Library Journal*. "Students tend to blithely accept that everything they see online is correct" (2000, p. 49).

With most students believing what they find online to be true, another troubling development is that students are clicking on a huge proportion of commercial webpages that have no bearing on their aca- demic objectives. This, of course, is not surprising, given the commer- cial nature of search engines (as explained in Chapter 3) or the com- mercial nature of the web in general. Communications scholar Samuel Ebersole (2000) has found that students select commercial sites much more than other domains:

> While students believe the WWW to be a valuable source of reliable
> information, their use of the WWW suggests other motivations.
> Analysis of sites visited indicated that by nearly a two-to-one margin
> students visited sites rated "unsuitable for academic research" ver-
> sus sites rated "suitable." Seeking out "pleasurable experience"
> appeared to win out over "learning information" when students
> were given access to the WWW within the school setting.

Furthermore, the types of sites visited most frequently, i.e., commercial sites, were rated as having the lowest educational value.

With students' high level of comfort with commercial search engines, with students' propensity to trust the many commercial websites visited via search engines, and with the bulk of commercial websites being unsuitable to their research, we are at an interesting crossroads in terms of the internet and education. How are educators and librarians dealing with what has now become a commercial highway in their classrooms?

SOLUTIONS TO THE COMMERCIAL CLUTTER

It is surprising that there has been so little concern about what has become of the number-one educational research tool for middle school, high school, and college students in the United States. Perhaps this is because most teachers and administrators seem to consider the web a neutral medium (with commercial annoyances). Perhaps educators don't bother about commercial inundation because they find commercial sites to be extremely useful to their students.

There have been a few bubbles of discontent over distracting, and sometimes inappropriate, online advertising (Reed, 1999). Some librarians have warned their colleagues about the presence of cookies on websites, which track users (e.g., Alexander & Tate, 1999). But if various educational and library trade journals are any indication of what educators are thinking, only a few published articles have discussed the growing number of commercial pages as a main contributor to internet clutter. Even fewer articles have made any connections between commercial search engines, the increase of commercial results in search engine lists, and the kind of material students are obtaining for their in-school research and homework. Arnold & Jayne (1998) and Brandt (1996b), for example, have commented on the savvy use of metatags ("keyword stuffing"), which then leads to skewed search results favoring sites with the highest numbers of descriptors. Kirk (2000) has mentioned the issue of paid placement, which prioritizes commercial pages. "Some search engines 'sell' top space to advertisers who pay them to do so," she writes, alluding to the high level of commercial sites that appear at the top of search engine lists, but not identifying the specific search engines involved in the practice (p. 2). Finally, Kennedy (1998) has warned against the commercially driven nature of search engines themselves, which display distracting advertisements, track user surfing habits, install cookies on people's hard drives, and impede the straightforward search for factual information. "Each individual search engine is desirous of being your best friend," she writes. "Why? For sure it's not a matter of virtual love. Each site wants you to visit as often as possible because high internet traffic is what attracts advertisers— and their wallets. (Ka-ching!)" (p. 22).

But these articles are rare in contemporary education and library discourse. When it really comes to website relevance, the major concern among educators and librarians are unfiltered (and therefore undesirable) personal homepages, which have no affiliation to any legitimate business or organization. Educators and librarians overwhelmingly see these "vanity" sites as imposters in the online environment; the pages almost selfishly clog up search engine lists with opinionated nonsense and are a main deterrent to students' finding "quality" information online. Solock and Wells (1999) typify this viewpoint:

> In a medium with no barriers to publishing, where anyone with an Internet connection, space on a computer server, and a rudimentary knowledge of HyperText Markup Language (HTML) can quickly create an Internet presence, it is very easy to "publish." Part of the great charm of the Internet is the ease with which anyone may have their say. However, from a librarian's point of view, particularly with respect to selection of quality resources, ease of publishing has a difficult flip side. It involves filtering through much information, often of dubious utility, to locate quality resources. (p. 208)

Accordingly, most educators have blamed ordinary people with time on their hands—or university students with personal agendas (and time on their hands)—for the "information explosion" and the high number of irrelevant webpages appearing on search engine lists. Graduate students come under particular scrutiny. As Safford noted in 1996, they have access to university servers, create personal sites, and then "get busy with other interests and simply desert their sites" (p. 43). The abandoned sites, she explained, continue to show up on search engine lists as dead links or as seriously outdated material. Nearly every article reviewed for this chapter noted the prevalence of suspect personal pages. This idea persists today despite evidence that the largest area of growth on the web is not from vanity publishers but from commercial enterprise, which already dominated 83% of the web in 1999 (Lawrence & Giles, 1999). Still, the problem exists that there is too much "bad information" online, and with students depending on and trusting the web for most of their academic research, numerous educators and librarians have concluded that students need help in finding applicable online content. Their solutions have generally fallen into four areas: subject gateways, power searching, webpage evaluation, and critical literacy.

THE CALL FOR SUBJECT GATEWAYS

Early on, both librarians and internet companies such as Yahoo!, which created one of the first commercial gateways to other sites, recognized the need to catalog and organize the internet. "We can either resign ourselves to terminal Information Anxiety or we can clean up the mess," Holt wrote in 1995. "Librarians and, especially, catalogers are uniquely qualified to tame the electronic wilderness—If not us, who? If not now, when?" (p. 34). Rosenfeld (1994), who taught at the University of Michigan's School of Information and Library Studies and founded one of the first nonprofit subject gateways (the Argus Clearinghouse), also wrote of the dire need for librarian input in internet categorization. Noting librarians' professional training in content evaluation, and in repackaging information in ways that enhance user access, Rosenberg said that the internet desperately needed these skills and that librarians were the obvious ones to evaluate and repackage the web.

Also called subject directories, subject trees, subject guides, or virtual libraries, these services—some commercial, many librarian-initiated—are attempts to pull related links together under specific topic headings. Emphasizing skilled human involvement and careful evaluation strategies, most subject gateways offer both hierarchies of topics and keyword searching. The document lists are manageable, and the selection process ensures that the sites have been evaluated—at least in some way—and annotated by real people. Yahooligans!, for example, is a subject gateway service that steers its K–12 audience to increasingly narrow subject categories and, finally, links to webpages that were preevaluated by an editorial staff. While the aim behind numerous services is to cover a broad swathe of categories (in an effort to be "all-inclusive"), some of the best subject gateways are extremely specialized, reflecting the topic areas of a distinct subfield and maintained by experts whose intent is to share the web resource with colleagues in their field. These gateways often remain hidden from general users, never reaching a wider public audience. More simplistic and assignment-oriented gateways are often established by teachers or school librarians who have searched sites on their own and then organized them on a printed sheet or, for more ambitious instructors, on a school-based homepage. These lists of links structure a student's web experience according to specific school assignments (Arnold & Jayne, 1998), sending them straight to previewed web content without potentially wasting time using search engines.

A handful of librarians see internet cataloging as central to the current and future work of all libraries and envision a nationwide and even global collaboration of resources (e.g., Holt, 1995; Kirkwood, 1998). Subject gateway efforts in the United Kingdom and in continental Europe have made significant inroads in this area, with a clear focus on higher learning. Britain, for example, has devoted consequential government funds toward the creation of interlinking subject directories and internet databases, the goal being to "transform the use and storage of knowledge in higher education institutions" (Resource Discovery Network, 2003). In the United States, existing efforts to catalog the web have developed either at a commercial level (e.g., Yahoo!) or among librarians and academics at a grassroots level, with often singular people organizing internet databases as stand-alone projects that are often spearheaded by national grants or university initiatives. Examples of these efforts include the Internet Scout Project (based at the University of Wisconsin), the Internet Public Library (based at the University of Michigan), the Librarian's Index to the Internet (an official part of the California Public Library), INFOMINE (based at the University of California), and the Merlot Project, which draws upon university professors across the United States.

To date, these numerous nonprofit internet cataloging projects across the United States have not been unified into a national public network, for a number of reasons. First, unlike the governments of the United Kingdom, the rest of Europe, or Australia, the U.S. government has made only halfhearted efforts to sponsor, promote, or protect subject gateway initiatives across the country. Dependent on voluntary help, those engaged in nonprofit cataloging efforts often have trouble keeping afloat and figuring out where to spend their limited funds—on cataloging or on self-promotion. "While recognizing that it is a professional responsibility to find, evaluate, and catalog internet information," Hinman and Leita (1999) write, "there are few individual public librarians who have either the time, dedication, or skills to do more than put a few links on the branch homepage" (p. 146). Indeed, the state of librarian-supported subject gateways in the United States is fragmented, and their survival is at risk (Hinman & Leita, 1999; Oder, 2000).

Second, commercial services, as I describe in Chapter 3, have already made inroads into the educational subject gateway scene. Directories such as Yahoo!, and ones that are specifically geared toward the K–12 market, such as AOL@School, heavily promote their subject gateway services, and, at least in the case of AOL@School, aggressively court K–12 administrators to get the service in schools (O'Leary, 1998). Many teachers regularly rely on Yahoo!'s "filtering" tools and give the service high marks, according to Paul & Williams (1999). "We love Yahoo!, too," they write. "It is often the first place we go when we're looking for a specific site or for a list of some good resources in a particular category" (p. 2). They are quick to note, however, that the commercial nature of Yahoo! and its paid placement practices have diluted its mission as a selective directory to quality resources. It is this commercialization that fuels the fire for Steve Mitchell and Margaret Mooney, who are behind the University of California's nonprofit INFOMINE directory. Arguing that subject gateways staffed with experts from within a given field or with knowledgeable librarians have a better chance of giving niche sites the proper attention they deserve, they are committed to providing "a public-domain academic finding tool that will remain free or inexpensive to use in the future" (1999, p. 105).

For all these reasons, at least in the United States, calls for using nonprofit subject gateways instead of their commercial counterparts exist only at the margins of education and library discourse. Most educators concerned about quality web content for the K–12 community do not even distinguish between nonprofit and commercial subject guides. As noted earlier, most educators are content to use commercial search engines, seeing them as the best and most efficient way to locate online information.

As valuable as subject gateways are as repositories of specialized, often noncommercial information, they face many challenges in gaining widespread use. Users in general don't trust their ability to stay current amid the ever-changing web environment, or their ability to be comprehensive. Potential users also don't know about them. Or, they prefer the simple ease of typing a single search term into a commercial search engine. None of this is very surprising to the editor of *Ariadne*, an online digital library journal out of the United Kingdom. "Librarians have known for years that a common characteristic of most new students is that they know almost nothing about libraries and how they work. . . . Google is an easy solution if you don't know what it can't find for you" (Hunter, 2002).

POWER SEARCHING

With a single search engine term capable of gleaning millions of hits, many librarians and educators hope to combat information overload by teaching students advanced searching skills. One strategy involves a better knowledge of Boolean operators—the searching techniques developed for library databases that have been adopted by a number of search engines. Kohut (2000), for example, refers to the benefits of "advanced search syntax":

> For more-advanced searches, use MetaCrawler's and SavvySearch's advanced search syntax, which helps refine your search so you can get better results. For instance, to designate groups of words in your search, enclose them in quotation marks (e.g., "George Washington"). You can also specify words or phrases that must appear in documents by prefixing them with a plus sign (e.g., "George Washington" +president), and also specify words or phrases that must not appear by prefixing them with a minus sign (e.g., "George Washington" –Carver). (p. 19)

Student confusion and the number of hits generated in broad searches can be minimized, then, by helping students understand that refined search terms can make an enormous difference in locating relevant websites. Salpeter (2003) even recommends that students compete to see who can find a piece of online information with the least amount of hits. "As your students work on refining their search skills," she writes, "take the opportunity to discuss what you have learned" (p. 23).

Besides stressing that students know how to refine search terms within any given search engine, numerous educators suggest that students should develop efficient ways to organize their searches and develop a better knowledge of differences between individual search engines. In their article "Fishing the Net," for example, Bailey and Lumley (1999) explain that "some [search engines] send robot software to every site and record the full text of every page. Others analyze the addresses in the database to determine which sites seem most popular (typically by determining the number of links pointing to the sites)" (p. A20). By considering each search engine as a unique tool with particular "search logics," and by trying more than one search engine when exploring a given topic, Bailey and Lumley, along with other researchers, argue that smart searching can better pinpoint quality information.

Educators and researchers who support power searching generally do not describe search engines beyond the way they build databases, determine relevancy, or match search criteria. They also do not distinguish between the impartial search technology and web indexes (supplied by search engine providers such as Inktomi and Google), search engine portals that are powered by such technology (such as Yahoo!, MSN, and Lycos), or commercial search providers (such as Overture). While Kirk (2000) has noted the practice of paid placement, and Kennedy (1998) has discussed consumer-profiling schemes among search engines (with both authors telling their readers to be wary of such practices), there are no attempts among educators to define the role of a commercial search provider or identify which search engine portals are the worst offenders. For the most part, those who advocate a better knowledge of search engines describe them as neutral tools, without considering the economic and commercial role that search engines play in the overall internet environment—a role that can heavily influence the number and variety of search results despite the best attempts to winnow the list.

WEBPAGE-EVALUATION SKILLS

Promoting information literacy has emerged as the most popular way to help students deal with the crush of websites. The goal, basically, is to help students critically interpret internet information—identify which sites are high quality (i.e., fact based and truthful) and which sites are low quality (i.e., misleading and irrelevant). These discerning skills are often referred to as the tools of "critical thinking," an umbrella term that is loosely applied to a range of higher-order thinking skills with regard to reading and producing texts. While critical-thinking skills have long applied to print texts, a number of educators believe that the web—as the host of so many varied and incongruent resources—calls for higher-level thinking capabilities. To many, the web also offers the perfect platform with which to help students understand the relevance of critical thinking. Arnold and Jayne (1998), for example, write that the web mixes the "useful and useless," thus giving teachers the chance to effectively teach the research process. Gardner and colleagues (1999) call this opportunity a "blessing" for English teachers who are trying to teach higher-level thinking. And Mather (1996) discusses the importance of exposing students to "raw, unfiltered, even contradictory information" so as to challenge their quest for credible sources, but also to arm students against less-than-credible information:

> The critically literate reader will be armed with the skills necessary to avoid the pitfalls of specious advertising, pseudo-science, narrowed reality (e.g. Holocaust revisionism, Scientific Creationism, cults), get-rich-quick schemes (time-share scams, pyramid schemes, innumerable mail frauds), political rhetoric, indoctrination, media bias, double-speak, twisted statistics, and other ills that prey on the gullible in this information society we live in. (p. 2)

The single, dominant theory of new information literacy within this particular body of literature can thus be summarized as follows: Students develop critical-thinking skills by determining whether a web text is high quality and "truthful" or low quality and "not truthful." These skills can then be translated to critically analyze other media. In order to help students find the truth on the web, a basic set of webpage evaluation criteria has been advanced in educational and library circles to this end. Borrowing from the already established librarian evaluation code for print resources—checking for authorship, accuracy, objectivity, currency, and coverage—librarians and educators have adapted these categories to the web for evaluating individual pages.

Authorship

Educators and librarians seem to agree that identifying website authors is one of the most important considerations to make when evaluating a website. With an overriding concern that "anyone can publish," questions have regularly revolved around establishing a single author's specific identity (e.g., Harris, 1997; Richmond, 1998) and testing this author for various credentials and levels of expertise. Gardner and colleagues (1999), for example, suggest that students locate an address, phone number, or email somewhere on the site—the ability to contact an author, they argue, helps to legitimize author credibility. Smith (1997) advises that links to biographical information are a good way to measure credibility, while others urge students to type the author's name into a search engine and see what other documents come up under the author's name (e.g., "Information," 1996). Ormondroyd, Engle, and Cosgrave (2000) suggest that students consult *Who's Who in America* or a biography index in order to establish author expertise. Additional authorship-verification strategies include determining if the information on the page is peer-reviewed or filtered ("Quality," 1999); if the site is a link from a "trustworthy" site (Kirk, 2000); if the source holds up against other sources (Brandt, 1996a; "Information," 1996); if the author relies on other reputable sources in a bibliography (Kirk, 2000; Reynolds & Plucker, 1999); and if it's possible to verify the identity of the webpage's server (Kirk, 2000).

Sponsorship is a key issue relating to authorship identity. Students are advised to find out if the webpage is sponsored by an organization, determine if the organization is "legitimate," and identify the domain under which the webpage is categorized. "Categorizing a site by its domain name—.com, .edu, .gov, .mil, .net, .org, or .us, for example—can send readers in the right direction to determine credibility," Bailey and Lumley (1999) write, "although it is only a first step" (p. A21). With this strategy, a .com website is considered slightly suspicious because it's likely to market a certain product or point of view, and thus may have a profit motive in relating information (e.g., Alexander & Tate, 1999), while .gov and .edu sites are considered information rich. Not all .edu sites, though: Like sleuths with an important discovery to share, many librarians and educators warn their readers about the potentially deceptive tilde (~) that is often affiliated with a "legitimate" university or educational site, but indicates that a single person with little authority is behind the information. Henderson's (2000) warning is typical: "If you see a tilde (~) as part of the URL, be aware that the website is a personal page likely created by someone who was given space on the web server in an unofficial, unauthorized capacity" (p. 2). The popular internet education newsletter *Classroom Connect* (published by a company that develops web-based curriculum products) printed this warning in 1996:

> A legitimate information provider will have a straightforward online address, such as http://www.xyz.com. On the other hand, an individual user will have an online address reading something like http://www.xyz.com/~sjm/data.html. The ~sjm part of the address gives it away. In this case, an individual with the initials SJM has put Web pages in his or her personal Web directory, and made their contents available to the world. (p. 4; see Appendix A)

Once again, these warnings lead back to the overriding emphasis throughout educational and librarian discourse that ordinary people (i.e., graduate students, misguided professors) are presumably responsible for disseminating the lion's share of misinformation on the web, not more "legitimate" sites such as "www.xyz.com." As a piece of advice, tilde warnings, while incredibly popular throughout the educational discourse, are actually a flimsy and simplistic way to judge author validity, especially since any "ordinary person" can also buy a top-level .com, .org, or .net domain name for about $35 a year—through domain name registration services such as Register.com or Networksolutions.com. Perhaps a more instructive way to determine sponsorship—and some educators are now advocating this—is to send students to the "About Us" or "Company Info" pages that appear on nearly every organizational, educational, government, or corporate site (Salpeter, 2003). Perhaps more effective than any other authorship/sponsorship investigation strategy, these pages are one of the surest ways to determine behind-the-scenes information about a website—its core mission, the individual spokespeople affiliated with the site/organization, press releases, annual reports (and addresses to shareholders), multiple levels of sponsorship, and even ulterior motives for the site's existence (which may affect or compromise web content).

Accuracy

In this third major category of webpage evaluation, librarians and educators point to the presence of typos, grammatical and spelling errors, and shoddy page design as a red flag against webpage quality (e.g., "Quality," 1999). Others consider the literary composition within a given webpage (e.g., Grassian, 2000; Ormondroyd et al., 2000) and ask questions concerning the level of balance and depth evident in the writing (Harris, 1997; Henderson, 2000), the legitimacy of a research method (Kirk, 2000), the general accuracy of the information ("Quality," 1999), and the provision of sources along with statistical material (Gardner et al., 1999). Reynolds and Plucker (1999) simply ask students to question whether time was put into the site, writing that "the overall attention to detail on the site is an indicator of content quality" (p. 12).

Objectivity

Measuring webpages according to an objective standard is a fourth criteria used for webpage evaluation. Ideal pages, most educators and librarians feel, should contain factually verifiable information, no verifiable bias (i.e., arguments should establish at least two sides of an issue) and clear distinctions between advertisements and information. When pages contain advertising, commercial gimmicks, or attempts to sway opinion, librarians and educators offer tips to students and teachers for judging potentially biased content more stringently. Alexander and Tate (1999), for example, differentiate between advocacy advertising, institutional advertising, corporate sponsorship, and nonprofit sponsorship and, in particular, warn about the subtle blending of information and advertising on many webpages, a practice, as noted in Chapter 3, which is becoming increasingly common. "On the Web, it is often not so readily apparent when an individual or group is supplying both the informational and advertising content of the page," they write. "Whenever any site accepts advertising and sponsorship but also provides information, the user must be aware of the potential influence by the advertiser or sponsor on the objectivity of that information" (p. 27).

Although Reynolds and Plucker (1999) discuss the presence of advertising, they do not see it as a sure sign of bias. Instead, they rightly note that many information-rich sites use ad revenue in order to make the site's availability and upkeep possible—the *New York Times'* online site, or *Salon* magazine, are examples of ad-supported informational websites. The advice, then, is to distinguish between the types of ads used on particular sites. "The type of ad can be an indicator of content quality (e.g., an educational site with ads for nightclubs is questionable; a site sponsored by the local PTA or a national distributor of teaching materials is probably not)" (p. 12).

Currency

This fourth category involves determining when the page was last updated. A recent update, according to webpage evaluation discourse, indicates that the website's information is well maintained and therefore more reputable. Gardner and colleagues (1999) ask, for example, "Is the date of the latest revision clearly stated? Is the date given for when the information was gathered? Is the page kept current? Are the links current—do they work? Is this truly the latest information on the topic?" (p. 41). In recalling Safford's complaint about graduate students who "simply desert their sites" (p. 43), one surmises that, once again, graduate students (or any unauthorized person not maintaining information on a webpage) are seen as the most typical culprits in lowering the overall value of the web.

Coverage

Finally, educators and librarians want students to consider the scope and depth of a particular site. If the site compares well to other sites (e.g., Grassian, 2000), contains supportive evidence for any conclusions (e.g, Henderson, 2000), covers the topic comprehensively (e.g., Ormondroyd et al., 2000), and offers links to other "legitimate" sources (e.g., Gardner et al., 1999), then, educators advise, the website gets high marks for quality.

As early as 1996, the widely circulated technology newsletter *Classroom Connect* published a "how to" guide to webpage evaluation, which documented the criteria listed above and offered a worksheet for teachers to copy and pass out to their students, who would apply the criteria to each page they visited. "If a student follows these steps," the newsletter's writer claimed, "they'll find that separating the good online information from the bad is a rewarding, enlightening experience" ("Information," 1996, p. 4). Since then, numerous librarians and educators (often university professors in education) have posted webpage evaluation checklists online. Librarians are incorporating these strategies in their orientations, and teachers, many teaching English, are designing research units around webpage critiques, many using the *Classroom Connect* guide as their resource. The hope is that once students learn to patiently proceed through the evaluation process with every web search, often using a checklist or question sheet as a guideline, and working within carefully constructed assignments, they can gradually internalize the fine points of webpage evaluation and eventually evaluate pages without any help (e.g., Bos, 2000; Scholz-Crane, 1998). Through these efforts, educators believe, they can better combat undiscerning students and information overload.

Moreover, they believe they can transform students into effective critical thinkers, not just in the way they address web content, but in the way they regard all information resources.

Although webpage evaluation practices are increasingly common among librarians and teachers, there is some evidence that they are not wholly effective. One issue is that students aren't bothering to use the webpage evaluation skills educators are teaching, and continue to rely on questionable information for their fact-supported, objective-style reports. For example, Arnold and Jayne (1998) observed that despite various efforts to teach students basic discerning skills, their students persisted in either not remembering these lessons or simply not applying them, using, in one particular instance, an online student paper as a credible source. "The process of identifying who is responsible for a Webpage and of verifying their credentials may require extensive investigation that consumes too much time," they noted. "Consequently, freshmen are often willing to accept the information without questioning the source" (p. 47). According to Gibson and Tranter (2000), "Comparing information with other [web] sources in a broad sense is indeed a tenable approach for differentiating between true and false information" (p. 2).

Watson (2001) reported a different problem. Students, she observed, are nervous about evaluating webpages when they are unfamiliar with the topic they are investigating. In other words, without prior knowledge of the subject they are researching, they feel ill equipped to identify what the most factual information is. "When one finds dates conflicting or other small errors, one is wary of the site as a whole," she reports. This problem is aggravated, Watson continued, by the large number of obviously biased material online.

As if discerning quality sites isn't hard enough, another difficulty is that many websites do their best to seem as unbiased as possible. Indeed, a web design aesthetic has evolved for most professionally crafted websites that incorporates *all* the webpage evaluation criteria outlined above. All organizations and corporations today use the web, in part, as a tool for public relations and have adopted a "credibility aesthetic" to appear as legitimate as possible to any reader. Their websites routinely list, for example, page "authors" and contact information. The pages are frequently updated. The information is written and copyedited by professionals, so typos and grammatical incongruities are rare. They provide bibliographic references to objective (or at least, objective-seeming) sites and articles. They present a balanced-sounding argument and even post website awards, no matter how bogus, that may increase the chances of the webpage *appearing* legitimate or objective. These evaluative criteria, for example, do little to prevent a student from thinking a public relations page with a well-crafted design and the aesthetics of objectivity in place provides valid and factual information, when its purpose is purely propaganda. As we have seen, students are often impatient web searchers; they also may corroborate one invalid website with another and feel that they are dealing with completely legitimate information all along.

CRITICAL LITERACY AND THE WEB

Some educators believe that a way to address these problems—and to alter the way students do web research—is to acknowledge that bias exists everywhere, that all information is couched in ideology, and that it's pointless to constantly search for "the truth" or for valid web information. Accordingly, they advocate changing assignments. Rather than asking students to write a paper or design a project based upon "true" facts gleaned from the web, literacy scholars such as Allan Luke (2000), Carmen Luke (2000), Julie Frechette (2002), Elizabeth Birr Moje and colleagues (2000), and James Paul Gee (2000) argue that students should address the world of opinion, not malleable facts. They have introduced an expanded form of literacy that positions all discourse within a political, economic, and social framework. In their view, fact-based assignments that lead to objective-style reports do little to help students understand more meaningful issues that directly or indirectly correspond to their social world: how political, economic, and social context shapes all texts, how all texts can be adapted for different social purposes, and how no text is neutral or necessarily of "higher quality" than another. In other words, the writers see no point in trying to determine the factual or "true" nature of certain information, but instead see the importance of understanding all information within a broader cultural context. This understanding, to these scholars, is the point of critical literacy. In Allan Luke's (2000) words:

> The aim of critical literacy is a classroom environment where students and teachers together work to (a) see how the worlds of texts work to construct their worlds, their cultures, and their identities in powerful, often overtly ideological ways; and (b) use texts as social tools in ways that allow for a reconstruction of these same worlds. (p. 453)

Under this notion of critical literacy, webpage-evaluation skills are a good first step in understanding a text's orientation. But rather than label a specific webpage "good" or "bad," critical literacy sees the page as the product of a particular context within a particular political and economic framework. As such, "raw, unfiltered, and contradictory information" doesn't necessarily challenge critical literacy, as Mather (1996) suggests, but enables it: Disparate sources (representing various contexts) invite students to acknowledge the "technical characteristics, social functions, and contexts of texts" (Luke, A., 2000, p. 453). In other words, students don't only learn information; they learn about and through information (see Cervetti, Pardales, & Damico, 2001, for an explanation of the differences between critical reading and critical literacy; Lankshear, Snyder, & Green, 2000). They learn how all information falls on a political and ideological continuum.

Australian education scholar Cushla Kapitzke (2001) offers a practical way of introducing this kind of critical literacy to students, teachers, and librarians working with web information. Instead of being consumed by the search for factual and credible information, teachers and librarians would do the opposite: construct and support assignments that ask for a range of theoretical, ideological, and political perspectives:

> Take, for example, the topic of globalization. Rather than seek the facts or the truth about its negative or positive impacts, student reading and analysis could focus on the social construction of discourses and practices of economic and cultural integration, which have costs and benefits, and advantages and drawbacks, in specific local and global contexts. In collaboration with the teacher, the cybrarian would furnish print and electronic texts produced by unionists, transnational corporations, indigenous peoples, feminists, environmentalists, and the World Trade Organisation, all of which would present different and often conflicting versions of "reality." Opportunity to analyse how these positions are materialized in language and text would show students that the production of knowledge necessarily entails relations of power that are able to be contested and transformed. Considering the power of information networks to connect and disconnect, and to include and exclude . . . , any pedagogy that ignores the political economy of information does a disservice to students, irrespective of whether they are part of and contributing to, or disconnected from, the electronic current of the Information Age. (pp. 453–454)

Kapitzke's vision of using information incorporates some elements of the web evaluation/checklist method but goes beyond it by asking students to acknowledge the shifting terrain of knowledge construction and work to synthesize their own opinions. Organizing opinions is very different from reporting facts. Salpeter (2003) also recommends that students work with contradictory webpages to understand numerous points of view:

> You could challenge students to do their own research to find point-counterpoint sites on such topics as the effects of television viewing on children or the advantages and disadvantages of a diet high in carbohydrates—or any other controversy that ties in with a current curriculum topic. As each site is located, students can summarize the key points being made and identify which ones directly contradict what they have learned elsewhere. Then it's time to debate what is the "truth." Which point of view is more popular? Does that make it more believable? Who created each site, and what reasons might that individual or organization have for espousing a particular point of view? Are they simply stating their opinion, or is there evidence that they are distorting or hiding information to make their case? (p. 22)

In teachers' helping students interpret contradictory online information, students could also investigate contradictions within a single website. They could deep link into the "About Us" sections of many corporate and organizational webpages, not to verify authorship, but to understand the often incongruous messages directed at a company's various audiences: shareholders (e.g., annual reports, press releases), potential advertisers (e.g., commercial opportunities), employees and potential employees (e.g., job listings), and the target audience of the website itself (homepage) (Fabos, 2000). One of the unique things about the web is that this type of "About Us" insider information is so readily available. Asking students to read the fine print of website privacy policies—what the policies are and how they may be subject to change—could provide another valuable lesson in understanding how the web's interactivity promotes a two-way information exchange: A website offers information but also expects its readers to divulge their own personal information in return.

Asking educators to require students to chart ideas rather than document truths is a rather new concept in education. This teaching strategy would work best if a student had access to as many varied ideas as possible. Given the scope of search engine corruption, and the tremendous hold that corporate public relations and commercial enterprise increasingly wields over the internet medium, however, this kind of many-viewpoint utopia is becoming increasingly hard to find. As we have seen in Chapter 3, all search engines except Google are exploiting user trust and manipulating search results to favor paying customers. The web is so commercially stacked that even Google—the sole search engine with content integrity—is not exempt from these powerful forces. At present, most educators are either concerned about information clutter (they advocate subject gateways, power searching, and webpage-evaluation skills) or creatively utilize the web's breadth of contradictory viewpoints (they endorse critical literacy). However, the teachers and librarians in both groups still view the whole internet in neutral terms—as a new technology owned by no one and free for anyone with internet access to use (or abuse). In their view, the "neutral" web environment, which changes only in terms of proliferating information, is host to a variety of suspicious, low-quality, or opinionated information that exists regardless of what impartial search engine is used.

Another level of critical literacy needs to be introduced that looks at the entire worldwide web as a complicated and contested text. In attempting to understand this text—this information resource—students would have to investigate the history of the medium, the various methods that search engines and subject gateways use to increase revenues, and many other commercial components of the web. What points of view, for example, are missing or hard to find? What areas of the web are silent, and why? It's one thing to understand that contradictory viewpoints coexist; it's another to understand why (and how) certain kinds of information, such as commercial speech, are privileged over other kinds. These discussions are not currently evident in the academic or public discourse on web content. Critiquing the web in its entirety can be difficult, however, because it points to questions about the existence of the web in education in general and raises issues about democracy within the context of capitalism. These are topics that, in many cases, educators are not willing to touch.

CHAPTER 5

A View from the Inside

I think I'm like everyone else here . . . I'm immune to it. The only time I ever go to advertising is if I accidentally click on it. So, I think [students are] much the same way.

—Ted Rockenbrodt, 9–12th grade social studies teacher, 2001

I'm basically immune to it.

—Seb, eighth grader, 2001

In the previous chapter, I reported the ways that so many educators and librarians across the United States and elsewhere are working to help students navigate the web, make their searches worthwhile, and develop ways to think more critically about web content. These educational trends have also been documented in countless books, articles, and studies. But for me, reading was not enough in my effort to assess the state of a commercialized internet in U.S. education. I wanted to see for myself what was going on in schools. And what I found, in my opinion, was a good deal of excellent teaching. In the very wired school district that I investigated for a year, I found that many teachers were using the internet extensively, requiring internet use by their students, and most important, helping them both conduct rewarding online searches and evaluate what they found. Moreover, a number of teachers were approaching the web in ways that were far more sophisticated than anything I had read about up to that point. There were many exciting aspects to my observations.

Although I witnessed what I considered to be very positive and commendable instruction, the story in this chapter is not all happy. The students I observed—as capable as they obviously were—did not choose to follow much of their teachers' good advice. In this sense, my investigations corroborate much of the trends elaborated in Chapters 3 and 4: Students use search engines for most of their school-related projects and persist in using them poorly, no matter what level of instruction. Meanwhile, they are inundated by commercial information, which either bogs down their searching or ends up in their final projects. In this chapter I detail my observations of school internet use from the inside of a Midwest school district.

WELCOME TO WALNUTVILLE

Walnutville is not the real name of the city where I conducted my investigation. To protect the identities of the teachers and students in my study, I changed all their names, as well as the name of the town. (Walnutville seemed midwestern enough [there are lots of walnut trees in the Midwest], and besides that, I happened to live on Walnut Street at the time I worked on this project.) Walnutville has about 35,000 people and is part of a metropolitan area of about 110,000. The city has three elementary schools, two junior high schools, and one high school. With impressive citizen and state support for large-scale school technology investment, computers and internet technologies are abundant in Walnutville. All elementary schools, both junior high schools, and the senior high school had a *minimum* of one linked computer in each classroom by 2000. Most had four to five per classroom, which was far above the national average. There were also significant numbers of computer labs, which is where most of my observations took place.

I was interested in observing children ages 8–17 (kids who were just learning to surf as well as the more experienced teen users), so I picked the most technologically rich of all the elementary schools (Hillup Elementary), the more wired (only slightly) of the two junior high schools (Homer Junior High), and the city's one high school (Walnutville High School). To begin my research at the three schools, I sent out a survey to determine the most common ways teachers used the web (and also to identify the most internet-savvy teachers). About half of all the teachers in the three schools returned the survey, and they revealed that the internet mainly functioned as a library substitute in these three Walnutville schools. Other internet uses, such as telecommunication exchanges or webpage design, were a significant minority in comparison to projects asking students to do individual research—to surf for information about a topic of their choice. Sixty-one percent of responding teachers assigned in-class projects that involved individual research in a school computer lab, with every student doing research on a computer. So, in general, Walnutville students often surfed the web in pursuit of information on a self-selected topic and wrote up research papers or created some kind of poster/presentation using that information.

My next step was to find teachers/media specialists at these schools who most frequently used the web in their teaching and encouraged online search activities during class. I contacted and interviewed 15 teachers/media specialists who were particularly avid internet users. Of these 15 educators, I did additional in-depth research on four who taught specific internet units on online research: Jill Whitmore, the media specialist at Hillup Elementary; Jack Stroh and Miriam Lowell, who co-taught a technology elective at Homer Junior High; and Steve LeRouge, who taught English at the high school. Besides formally interviewing these four educators at least twice, I observed them in the classroom, observed their students' classroom research processes, and talked with them informally numerous times.

Finally, I interviewed a group of 21 students (selected from both Stroh and Lowell's and LeRouge's classrooms) as they conducted classroom online research. Using a "think aloud" method of interviewing, I videotaped students' computer screens to record their selections and talked to them to get them to verbalize their decisions as they surfed the web. Thus, I was able to visually document the choices they made as well as the surfing strategies they used. I supplemented all these observations and interviews with other student data: web critique assignments that the junior high and high school students had completed at one point during the semester and their other finished projects—the results of their in-class web research.

TEACHERS: IN SEARCH ENGINES WE TRUST

Based on my interviews with all the 15 teachers and media specialists, I found that nearly all regarded search engines as the most obvious and efficient way to find information on the worldwide web. They had faith that their students could find trustworthy informational sites related to a particular topic of study using search engines. They also, by and large, trusted their students' searching skills. Many used the word *savvy* to describe their students' search engine abilities and marveled at what they saw was an increasing dexterity with online material.

Sixth-grade teacher Melanie DeBower, for example, asked her students to search for online facts when she taught units on wetlands and famous people. Her students incorporated the information they found into HyperStudio (a presentation software that stacks pages and incorporates photos and graphics) and a written report, respectively. DeBower easily justified sending her students to search engines: most had computers at home and were already accustomed to conducting free-form searches on the web; others with less search engine experience could benefit from such activities. She also found that preselecting sites for her students was often prohibitively time-consuming on her end and that her students enjoyed being "set free" on the web.

Both ninth-grade English teacher Miriam Lowell and seventh-grade science teacher Joe Doherty also let their students search the web during class time, although they often asked their students to begin their searches by visiting a number of sites they chose ahead of time. For Lowell's Odyssey and Renaissance units, for example, she gave her students a handout containing specific URLs as a way to get them on the right track. "I give them a starting place; that's the way I phrase it," she said. "This is your starting place. Get into the links, at least two or three of the links you should be looking at, and then go from there." Similarly, Doherty directed his students to the NASA page or other government resources before letting them explore the web independently. Surfing, he explained, was an important lesson in and of itself:

> I do think that's important because some of our kids have
> vast amounts of experience with the Internet and some have
> none, and so I think it's important for them to have that
> opportunity and go on there and surf about, and we take a
> couple of days where I know that some time will be killed.
> Necessary evil I think. Just to get the experience of wander-
> ing around that great big vast array of information.

Jack Stroh, who with Miriam Lowell co-teaches an eighth-grade elective called Electronic Technology and Learning, was a particular advocate of free-form web surfing during class. To facilitate an even wider use of search engines, Stroh adjusted the internet portal in the school's Mac Lab (normally set to Yahoo!) so that a list of 21 search engines appeared on the screen with their accompanying logos. As the most technologically literate instructor in the junior high school, Stroh had faith in his students' ability to research diverse topics and find factual information by typing in applicable key words. He was encouraged by what he felt was his students' emerging web proficiency.

High school teachers in this study also tended to assign research projects that welcomed, and even required, web research. Of the five papers that English teacher Trina Matthews assigned over a given semester, four of them required her 11th/12th-grade students to use internet search engines and cite web sources in the papers. Biology teacher Dutch Hurley assigned two or three research papers a semester to his upper-level students. These projects were so integrated with the web that Hurley invited his students to design webpages, which incorporated links to relevant sites, in lieu of written papers. Social studies teacher Ted Rockenbrodt assigned multiple web research projects to his four U.S. History (9th and 10th grade) classes and his Developing Nations (11th and 12th grade) class. English teacher Steve LeRouge also assigned research papers that required in-class web research in both his advanced and lower-level English classes.

All these teachers—elementary, junior high, and high school—reserved time in one of the school's computer labs so that students could search the web for these assignments during class. Sometimes they collaborated with the school's media specialists, who facilitated student research projects in the media center when students visited during reserved class time or during free periods. "The Internet has just opened everything up," high school media specialist Karen Truax said. "I just think that students feel like there's little information that they can't find." For these educators, the worldwide web was a library of facts, and search engines were the most logical pathways to these facts.

Even as they embraced search engines, the teachers and media specialists I talked to fully recognized that much of the information available online was not appropriate for student viewing or relevant for fact-based assignments. Search engines were chaotic places and the lists they generated were as full of garbage as they were of useful information. The challenge for many of these educators, then, was to help students wade through a large number of websites and find the kind of unbiased and trustworthy information they needed to complete a fact-based research assignment. Educators generally had three strategies for doing this. First, at least for the lower grades, they did the search engine wading *for* their students, getting on search engines themselves and locating applicable sites to introduce in class. Second, they taught power-searching strategies to generate more relevant search result lists. And third (and by far most common), they taught webpage-evaluation techniques so that their students could better judge the validity and quality of individual webpages on their own.

Teaching Strategies: Subject Gateways

Only educators in the lower grades preselected sites, or turned to subject directories such as Yahooligans! Hillup's media specialist, Jill Whitmore, was perhaps the leading advocate of website preselection. She felt strongly that the web was too huge a database for elementary students to handle, and sending students all over the web on fact-finding missions was a waste of classroom time. Accordingly, she advised teachers to select quality sites ahead of time. Realizing that this could be time consuming, Whitmore offered to help by passing around a sheet once a month asking teachers to designate topic areas that she might investigate for them. Whitmore also advocated educational subject directories such as KidsClick, which was developed by K–12 media specialists, librarians, and educators. "We preview textbooks for kids," she said. "There's a whole selection criteria. We should be doing the same for websites." Whitmore was so bent on preselection that she was working on creating her own list of websites that could be accessed through the Hillup's online library database.

Third-grade teacher Judy Valencia had taken a cue from Whitmore and often searched for sites beforehand rather than let her students look for sites themselves. She had watched one of her students mistakenly open up a pornography site while doing research on Olympic figure skater Michelle Kwan, and from that point on decided to search for quality sites on her own. Like Whitmore, she also thought free-form searches wasted instructional time, but admitted that finding applicable sites for particular class units took *her* time (she had not yet relied upon Whitmore's assistance). Consequently, she often did not have enough hours in the day to do these searches. Valencia's alternative to preselecting websites was sending her students to "safe" subject direcories that offer lists of sites already prescreened by "content experts" or "academics" and organized into basic categories (e.g., art, education, science). Her directory of choice was Yahooligans!.

At the junior high level, eighth-grade English teacher Suzanne Rommel also felt more comfort in preselecting websites for her students, rather than letting them loose on search engines. Besides finding webpages herself for particular units (e.g., on the Holocaust and on certain authors), she was particularly pleased with her textbook, *Prentice-Hall Literature*, which suggests applicable URLs in her teacher's edition (not the student version). "It's all there; it's absolutely great for us," she said. "Here are the websites that you might go to and here's where you might find the answer." Although Rommel relied upon her textbook as a kind of directory to internet sites, she had little or no knowledge of online subject gateways such as Britannica.com or AOL@School. Indeed, only a few teachers I talked to at the junior high and high school level had heard of these services. Most felt they were not worthwhile or too elementary, preferring to send their students to search engines instead.

Teaching Strategies: Power Searching

Introducing students to "power searching" techniques was common at both the junior high and high school but not in the elementary school. *Power*, or *advanced*, searching refers to the use of Boolean operators (e.g., *and, or, not*) to more successfully narrow down a web search, and understanding the differences between various search engines (e.g., search engines vs. metasearch engines). In the eighth-grade elective Stroh and Lowell co-taught called Electronic Learning and Technology, they asked their students to complete an online tutorial that took them through the basic concepts of Boolean syntax as it related to the web. Students worked on the tutorial during one or two class periods (depending on how quickly the student learned that material) and took a graded quiz on the concepts they learned.

At the high school level, media specialists Karen Truax and Sandy Ingersoll explained Boolean strategies to all 10th graders at the beginning of the school year as part of their library orientation. They mainly applied this presentation to the school's subscription-based internet databases, available through the high school media center, although they also explained that the same methods could be used for many search engines. Some teachers later invited the school's media specialists to their class for a refresher session on Boolean search terminology and webpage critique strategies. English teacher Trina Matthews, for example, asked Truax and Ingersoll to talk to her 11th- and 12th-grade classes before they began working on their web research projects. English teacher Steve LeRouge also touched upon the basics of Boolean operators in his own classes and discussed a number of search engines he found to be the most useful (e.g., Sherlock and Google). Other teachers, such as social studies teacher Ted Rockenbrodt, felt confident that the sophomore library orientation was sufficient for their students and believed that their students applied Boolean strategies during their web searches at home and in school.

Teaching Strategies:
Evaluating the Web, Page by Page, by Page . . .

To many of the educators in my investigation, the web could be easily tamed—and could fulfill its promise as an educational resource—if students could learn to distinguish the good content from the bad. Following the liberal-humanist tradition of critical reading, which values truth, objectivity, and attempts to identify author intent (see Cervetti, Pardales, & Domico, 2001), a "good" webpage was one that offered straightforward, trustworthy, and factual information; a "bad" page was one that demonstrated obvious bias and had sloppy, misleading information. Educators generally felt that learning to wade through the "garbage" of any given web search also offered a means for learning critical-thinking skills; the more pages students had to wade through, the better their critical-thinking skills could become. With these skills, the web as an overwhelming database could be surmountable. As such, the majority of the teachers and media specialists I spoke to made admirable efforts to educate their students about the potential biases of various kinds of online materials and to distinguish between good and bad content. "Kids don't always know what's real and what's not," high school biology teacher Dutch Hurley remarked. "And I think that's good. Part of the whole learning process is that they have to sift through what's garbage and what's real."

Of the 15 educators I interviewed, 9 taught their students evaluation criteria outlined in the previous chapter—authority, accuracy, objectivity, currency, and coverage. Most teachers had gathered information for such discussions from education articles passed along to them at teaching conferences and at in-service internet workshops held by the local education agency—an indication of the pervasiveness of this discourse. This evaluation criteria put an emphasis on the individual web content author and his or her expertise in a given subject area. Not surprisingly, the educators I interviewed tended to highlight the notion that websites authored by ordinary people are the most likely sources for misinformation on the web and are responsible for making web searches so unwieldy and cluttered. Seventh-grade science teacher Joe Doherty was typical of the teachers I interviewed:

> I mean, anyone can put anything they want on the web. I can make up my own site and say, "I am the Ozone watchdog for the Midwest." I could make up some name and call myself some society, and I could put any cacamana on there—and I think I could and some people do!

Because "anyone can put anything on the web" (a phrase that kept recurring in numerous discussions I had with teachers and media specialists), the webpage-evaluation methods at Hillup, Homer, and Walnutville High placed a priority on establishing webpage authorship. At the elementary level, media specialist Jill Whitmore (and not the Hillup teachers themselves) handled such discussions for the school's fifth- and sixth-grade students. "We go through a checklist of criteria for a good site," she told me. "Is there an author, a creator? When was it last updated? Is it a .edu or a .com? Where is this person coming from? Do the links work?"

At the junior high and high school levels, class discussions about untrustworthy authors and their potential biases happened more frequently and spontaneously. For example, when both seventh-grade science teacher Doherty and high school biology teacher Dutch Hurley asked their students to investigate current scientific events online (projecting a certain webpage on a screen to generate class discussion), they would bring to the students' attention the dubious nature of some webpages. Describing his teaching, Hurley explained:

> We look at what's real science and what's not real science, and I incorporate some of the websites that we found by accident. Human cloning is a big one. There are millions of sites

out there that claim that they've cloned humans and if you send me $300 and some DNA I can clone you and stuff. And we look if this is real or if this is not.

High school English teacher Trina Matthews also referred to biased author pages in larger discussions about language use. In three of her upper-level composition classes, she had taken her students through a sample essay that presented itself as a factually based document. After highlighting words that indicated the writer's bias, she extended the lesson by stressing the ubiquity of biased resources online and the "misinformation on personal pages," which can contain similar language styles. Correspondingly, in his goal to have his students be "efficient users of the internet," high school social studies teacher Ted Rockenbrodt frequently interjected advice about domain names as his students were researching during class time, "so that they know if they go to Joe's Basement page, that's not where I want to be for valid information, whereas Tulane.edu, you're probably going to get some good stuff there." Generally, these educators deemed webpages that had no identifiable author but were created by a known organization or company (and looked professional) more sound and truthful than pages created by individuals. This practical standard relates to what I discussed in Chapter 4, what I call the "credibility aesthetic"—an aesthetic that satisfies many of the credibility criteria (e.g., contact information, good grammar) but may not necessarily be credible.

Some teachers developed webpage-evaluation units that spanned days or even weeks. For their eighth-grade elective Electronic Technology and Learning (a class that serves about 20 students each semester), Stroh and Lowell led lessons about the internet and web content that were quite remarkable in their depth. They developed a 3-week long unit called the Internet, which was broken up into sections called Terms and Concepts (email, the worldwide web, internet service providers), Web Page Evaluation (domains, author validity, metatags, link investigation), and Search Techniques (engines and directories, Boolean operators, metasearch, local sources). They taught "The Internet" in the first third of the fall 2000 semester. Stroh and Lowell assigned a significant amount of class time for the various activities, and students basically worked on their computers as the two teachers assisted individual students. The co-teachers worked from materials they had collected at the state's annual educational technology conference and from handouts from the area education agency. One article from the monthly newsletter *Classroom Connect* was particularly informative in their teaching: "Information Literacy and the Internet: How to Sort 'Good' Online Information From the Bad" ("Information," 1996). They also drew upon their own expertise. Stroh is a computer whiz who troubleshoots technology problems throughout the school; Lowell has taken courses on web design at the local university, and with an academic librarian for a spouse, she has a personal interest in information evaluation.

For their discussions devoted to the section Terms and Concepts, Stroh and Lowell worked to improve their students' understanding of the internet's different components—the technology behind the information tool. This in and of itself, I found, was impressive. As they moved to Web Page Evaluation, they were more typical at first, beginning discussions about authorship validity by defining domain categories, explaining their differences, and issuing warnings about certain URL addresses that could indicate misinformation or bias. For one class period, Lowell explained the individual domain categories (.edu, .com, .gov, .org, .mil., and .net). "You have a fighting chance if it's an .edu that the information will be accurate," Lowell said, and underscored that "safe" domains such as .edu can also be misleading and biased. To illustrate, she and Stroh highlighted the infamous webpage authored by Northwestern University professor Arthur R. Butz (pubweb.northwestern.edu/~abutz), who makes absurd claims that key events documented about the Holocaust didn't happen. Stroh and Lowell discussed the way authors can seem reputable on the outset (as in Butz's appearing on a university server), but espouse extremely biased points of view. An academic-sounding .edu site should not be trusted unconditionally, they warned, noting that a URL with a tilde is also an indication of a potentially untrustworthy page. (As I discuss in Chapter 4, warning users about tildes is a prominent theme in the current literature).

Like so many educators nationwide, Stroh and Lowell viewed sites designed by individual people—personal pages—with the most mistrust. They advised students to visit the online bookstores Amazon.com and Barnes&Noble.com to see if web authors had also published reputable books—a helpful way, in their view, to determine an author's legitimacy. They also discussed ways for their students to identify the type and number of external pages that chose to link into a particular site in question (e.g., go to the AltaVista search cell and type "link:" and the site's web address). A site was presumed to be more legitimate if numerous sites linked to it from their webpage (Google uses a similar strategy to determine relevance). Stroh and Lowell also told their students not to automatically exclude .coms as biased and opportunistic, and gave the example of a "beautiful and informative" page about the Sistine Chapel renovation that is sponsored by an air conditioner corporation charged with keeping the climate controlled for the renovation. Finally, they mentioned the page's currency, and whether or not a visitor could email the page's author, as markers of website legitimacy.

Finally, the two teachers introduced a section on search techniques, whereby they discussed various practical differences between search engines (which engines were Boolean friendly, which were not), had students go through a Boolean tutorial (described above), and showed students how to identify metatags that define a site (go to View-Source on the web browser to access the HTML code). For this component, Stroh and Lowell asked their students to consider the way a particular site positioned itself within the context of search engine searches.

This impressive instructional unit for the eighth-grade level went one step further, as Stroh and Lowell integrated their webpage-evaluation discussions with a number of small assignments meant to increase students' understanding of web domain categories. They asked students to email a commercial, noncommercial, and government website of their choice and see what kind of response (if any) they would receive; and they asked students to choose three out of five websites Stroh and Lowell had preselected under each of the six domain categories (.gov, .edu, .org, .com, .net, and .mil), follow at least two links to get a better sense of the overall site, and write brief summaries of the type of information they found. They also asked students to visit the Walnutville city website and review some of the listings they found there as a way to orient them toward the web's civic potential. Finally, Stroh and Lowell assigned timely reading selections drawn from current newspapers and magazines that centered on five topic areas they had identified about technology: privacy (censorship, copyright, personal freedoms); education (today's technology in education, global education); consumerism (e-commerce, savvy consumerism, gadgets, games and toys); society (careers, impact of technology on society); and the future (new technology, scientific or medical technology). "Both of us read journals on the Internet," Stroh explained, "and these were the issues we picked out that were the most common, that people were writing editorials about."

After the internet unit, Stroh and Lowell turned to a unit called Computer Graphics, which introduced students to digital cameras and other technology accessories. The third and final unit, Webpage Building, occupied the last month and a half of the semester. Students began the unit learning the basics of webpage design using a Claris Homepage tutorial. Then Stroh and Lowell assigned the class's final project: Students had to pick a topic that they had covered (or were about to cover) in another class and apply the web-researching and web-evaluation techniques they learned earlier in the semester to gather online information and visuals. They then had to use the information and graphics they found to be the most credible and build their own informational webpage. Stroh and Lowell also required that students document their web sources, define the web source's domain, write down the individual or group responsible for maintaining the site, and document what other sites linked to their source sites.

Combined with the work students did in the first Internet unit, all these exercises were meant to help students decide if the sites they chose for their research were valid and trustworthy. Indeed, this list of activities was both ambitious in scope and, based on my review of current educational practices, particularly unusual for the eighth-grade level. In subsequent semesters, Stroh and Lowell decided to place The Internet and Webpage Building closer together. According to Stroh, students had forgotten much of the power-searching and webpage-evaluation skills they had learned by the time they had a chance to apply them.

High school English teacher Steve LeRouge, like Stroh and Lowell, was especially committed to teaching his students webpage-navigation and -evaluation skills in his two advanced Comprehension and Perception classes. He had been teaching some form of webpage evaluation since 1996, and during the semester I observed his class he was teaching an entire unit on internet research. He introduced the unit by showcasing his favorite search engine portals (Sherlock and Google), reiterating power-search strategies, and outlining the various internet domains. The bulk of the unit, however, was spent on webpage-evaluation skills and was informed by the same *Classroom Connect* article used by Stroh and Lowell ("Information," 1996), as well as the online (now offline) document "It Must Be True, I Saw It on the Net: Real Research on the WWW," which LeRouge received at an area education agency workshop in 2000. Drawing upon the recommendations in this webpage-evaluation tutorial and his own web-researching experience, LeRouge spent an entire class period critiquing the webpage www.designer-drugs.com, which featured an article called "Future Synthetic Drugs of Abuse" and a list of pro-drug-related links. As his students simultaneously scrolled through the article and specific links on their individual computers, LeRouge pointed out various elements that deemed the article's author, and the webpage itself, either trustworthy or troubling. This is an excerpt of LeRouge's class lecture:

> If you look at this it seems pretty reputable. It seems to be set forward in a scholarly format, there's a nice solid title.
> There's a person, David A. Cooper, he has a pedigree, Drug Enforcement Administration, McLean, Virginia, yeah, the home of the [CIA]. So in fact you'll see that you also have an index at the very outset, and that particular index is basically a page where you can scroll up and down that page.
>   As you look at it then again it seems set up in pretty straightforward, almost scholarly fashion. You have the introduction that lists the hallucinogens, the subgroups to hallucinogens, stimulants, sedatives, etcetera. If you scroll down so you have the introduction in the middle of the page, I want to show you things that are seemingly pretty solid bits of information, and he introduces this, a kind of attractive prose style, kind of that quasi-scientific style, with a lot of passive verbs in it. You know—"It is determined"—those types of things.

LeRouge continued to illustrate how a seemingly scholarly, relatively current page (he showed his students how to determine currency by selecting "View" and "Page Info" on the browser) had some suspicious links: Future Opioids (http://opioids.com), a "pro-drug rant" that led to other people's rants about the orthodoxy of self-medication; the Good Drug Guide (http://biopsychiatry.com), which called itself "the responsible parent's guide to healthy mood-boosters for all the family"; and BLTC Research (http://www.bltc.com), which

promoted "paradise engineering" to "abolish the biological sub-
strates of suffering." Besides pointing out the pro-drug bias of the
webpage links appearing alongside this particular article, LeRouge
asked his students to do an author check on David A. Cooper by
inserting his name into the search engine Google (this was a strategy
similar to that of Stroh and Lowell, who recommended plugging a
webpage author into the Amazon.com database). Because the same
article (but none other) appeared on multiple sites, LeRouge illustrated how this author's name was potentially fabricated, or how the
author had less credibility than someone listed within the context of
a larger, known organization. "If you can't find anything else by
him," he said, "I would probably hesitate to use him as a major
source. I might use him as a secondary source, but not as a major
source." Like Stroh and Lowell in their focus on the Arthur R. Butz
website, LeRouge was directing his critique toward a single webpage
author who held a particular point of view. The currency of the website, and the presence of contact information, were also priorities in
determining the webpage's credibility. LeRouge's message was consistent with that of Stroh and Lowell: Webpage bias and misinformation is rampant on the web, and one has to be a sleuth in the search
for factual information.

LeRouge's Internet Research unit included two related assignments. First, he asked his students to conduct online (and other
library) research on a topic of their choice and write a fact-based
research paper using the information they found. Second, he assigned
an "Online Critique," a checklist of 13 questions, which students had
to apply to one particular webpage they had found for the topic they
were researching. The 13 questions came from the same *Classroom
Connect* newsletter ("Information," 1996), and were meant to help students differentiate between "good" and "bad" web content. For example, the handout asked students to consider authority, accuracy, objectivity, currency, and coverage and to compare the webpage with any
library materials they may have found (see Appendix A). LeRouge
scheduled three class periods in which students could conduct online
research and complete their web critique, which they had to write up
and hand in. As they worked, LeRouge spent these class periods visiting with individual students and continuously helping them sift
through the legitimacy of particular websites. In this particular discussion, LeRouge talked to one student researching Ritalin as they
both viewed the website http://www.breggin.com:

LeRouge: This guy has a clear bias, what's his clear bias?
Student: To keep kids off.
LeRouge: To keep kids off of Ritalin. OK? He's a medical doc-
    tor, it says M.D. Now we don't know if he's a general
    practitioner, we don't know if he's a family doctor, we
    don't know whether he's a podiatrist, for crying out loud.
    OK? "Founder of the International Circle of Study." OK,
    he's the founder . . . OK . . . that says something. . . . Where
    is this coming from. It's a .com. This is a good thing you
    might want to critique, because while [the text] says one
    thing, [the sponsorship] says another. What do you sup-
    pose that links to? Go ahead and click it . . . see what hap-
    pens . . . (reads). Let's see. Oh, make payment in dollars.
    Twenty-five bucks. So here is a question. If it's a nonprofit
    organization, right? It's going to send you a button, you're
    going to send them $25. How much does it cost to put up
    a webpage as an M.D.? Do you really think he can afford a
    webpage? So that's an interesting one. I would take it with
    a grain of salt. Again, some of the information may be
    interesting information that you may be able to check
    against other information that you get. But if you were to
    critique this site, you may want to make a point of saying
    what kind of information . . . does he have any links to any
    other sites, is there any bias to the author, you can say,
    "Yeah . . . " You might also ask, "Why is this information
    online?" You can say the guy put this information up to
    inform. On the other hand, he's also making money for a
    supposedly nonprofit organization and trying to encour-
    age membership. That's what I would do.

This student would later choose this webpage for his 13-question
Online Critique.

After all the students had completed their critiques and handed
them in, LeRouge visited with each of them individually as he
returned their papers. During these impromptu teacher-student sessions, LeRouge reiterated what he wrote down on their critiques: He
pointed out that a page that was not recently updated was suspect,
that nothing on the web should be trusted until the webpage and web
author satisfied numerous authorship, accuracy, objectivity, currency,
and coverage criteria and that commercial pages (.coms) featured

potentially compromised information. Even then, LeRouge recommended that the webpage be cross-listed and compared to other online information on the same topic, and he frequently suggested that students email the author for additional source ideas.

Teachers' Personal Views on the Web

As I have tried to illustrate, teachers regularly assigned web-based research projects in their classrooms in the Walnutville school district, and in some cases talked about internet technology and webpage evaluation strategies extensively. Teachers were generally concerned with information overload and with equipping their students so they could find the most useful sites. Some, like LeRouge, were concerned about helping their students read against the commercially biased content they encountered. But although teachers and media specialists were certainly annoyed by advertising, they didn't see banner ads as interfering with their students' research projects. "I don't know, you're living in America, you know, you're in a capitalistic society, and the kids are pretty savvy to that, in a way," one teacher remarked. "I don't think that they are unaware that everything comes with a little price tag and a little hook for advertising there."

Similarly, teachers at Walnutville were not overly concerned with the numerous online games and contests that attempt to extract personal information from players, mostly because they didn't see these issues as affecting in-school experiences. Hillup's media specialist Jill Whitmore did introduce her fifth and sixth graders to the concept of cookies. Indeed, she had adjusted the preferences in all the media center's computers so that students were constantly warned whenever a cookie was being sent. Whitmore wanted her students to know that computers may be monitored by outside entities via cookies and that it should be their decision what they wanted to show and whether to accept a cookie or not. (Of course, by not accepting a cookie, a user is often denied access to the site.) Stroh and Lowell had also discussed cookies and spam with their students during previous semesters, asking them to read articles on issues of junk mail and profiling. During the semester in which I observed Stroh and Lowell's class, they chose to focus on other technology issues.

Regarding search engine commercialization, most educators I talked to embraced search engines as the most effective and trustworthy means of finding quality web content, so there was little reason for them to critique such popular tools. "Usually they can find something worthwhile," one media specialist said, "even if it takes some extra time." Moreover, educators did not foresee search engines changing dramatically in the future, question search engine effectiveness (given the increasing number of webpages to sift through), or question the commercial nature of search engines as profit-seeking corporations. When asked to consider the likelihood of commercial influences on search engine result lists, the teachers I talked to were not aware of these developments and thus not concerned.

In fact, high school social studies teacher Ted Rockenbrodt believed search engines' navigation services would improve in time, with the increased competition between search engine sites. He explained, "I have full confidence in the private sector . . . that as we have more web-pages, they're going to have more sophisticated search engines." With better search engines (provided by the private sector), a sound knowledge of advanced power-search techniques, and good webpage-evaluation skills, Rockenbrodt believed students would be able to find the sites they were looking for. For him, the fact that the web was becoming more and more privatized was its biggest asset. He remarked:

> I think there is still going to be plenty of really good stuff out
> there for us to find. And whether they are prioritized, and
> whether it is the free enterprise system entering into it, I
> guess that's just part of it. But I still think we're going to find
> good stuff. . . . If we [teachers] can't find online documents,
> then we're not expecting them [students] to. We're probably
> not seeing what we're missing anyway. I suppose that's a
> defeatist way of looking about it, but . . .

In other words, Rockenbrodt believed noncommercial sites would either trickle down through the many commercial sites and personal pages, and if they didn't, it didn't matter—what we don't know can't hurt us.

If Rockenbrodt's assignments are any indication, he embraced the web as not much more than a vehicle for free enterprise. One research assignment he developed, for example, was meant to be a lesson in internet abundance: teaching students how so much information— made up of arcane details—was available online. The assignment was for his Developing Nations class, which he taught to 11th and 12th graders. Students had to pose as tourists/businesspeople and use the web to design an itinerary for a business trip to a South American country. In teams of three, they had to use search engines to locate "facts" about car rental prices, restaurants, hotels, travel, and a company that paralleled their chosen business interest. Students found, for example, that in Brazil, a Ford Explorer rents for $60 a day, the Pizza Hut in Rio doesn't serve forks with their pizza, a luxury hotel in downtown Rio includes an American continental breakfast with the room price, and that tourists can ride mountain bikes through the Amazon EcoPark. "Kids love to do this," Rockenbrodt said. "They love to search." Indeed, as I watched them work in pairs in the computer lab, I observed students enjoying themselves as they investigated their developing nations. One conversation I overheard went as follows: "Do we all want to stay in the room together, or have separate rooms?" "Oh, I think separate rooms would be OK." "Oh look, we can reserve a suite of rooms!" Meanwhile, Rockenbrodt urged his students to bolster their itineraries with more and more minute facts. "I don't want you to print off a bunch of crap from the Internet and hand it in," he said. "I'm looking for detail. Find all the things, present it nicely, and show me what I need to see." Since Rockenbrodt's students were asked to locate facts that by and large concerned commercial enterprise, they had no problem finding the information for which they were looking. Car rental agencies, hotels, and restaurants such as McDonalds—all would have high-profile websites. But Rockenbrodt did not provide a framework for understanding the web as a commercial medium beyond the notion that lots of commercial information was indeed available online.

Rockenbrodt's complete confidence in the internet as a commercial educational medium was an extreme case. Other teachers were more contemplative of the future of the internet as a mass medium and its evolving role in education. Seventh-grade science teacher Joe Doherty, for example, initially saw the web as a decentralized medium that would remain essentially democratic, safe from commercial domination, and, therefore, navigation tools such as search engines would be nonproblematic. He argued that all perspectives would eventually trickle down and through the web, and he remarked, as did Rockenbrodt, that commercial forces would never succeed in effectively distorting the information flow—that some countervailing force would always prevent that from happening. However, when Doherty began comparing the internet to television and cable industries, which are dominated by corporate oligopolies, his argument began to change. In acknowledging that there are very few television programs that are critical of corporate or media culture, he also acknowledged that a privatized internet may also limit critical discussions about the economic, political, and cultural issues that are crucial for democracy. In making these connections, Doherty observed that despite numerous for-profit educational initiatives, "the best educational sources [on the internet] are from educators."

Doherty wasn't the only teacher I talked to who was grappling with the internet as a commercial entity and with commercial search engines as the obvious tools for searching that entity. High school biology teacher Dutch Hurley, who was one of the many who saw the value of students' "sifting through garbage" to enhance critical-thinking skills, also noticed his students wasting too much time searching for usable websites in his classroom. For certain kinds of assignments, at least, Hurley was beginning to think that subject directories, carefully prepared by educators, would be more useful to him and his students than search engines.

Jill Whitmore, Hillup's media specialist, took this notion one step further. If Rockenbrodt represented one end of the continuum—utter faith in commercial search engines and glowing praise for the internet as a privatized mass medium—Jill Whitmore represented the other end: She mistrusted the web as a commercial medium and was doing something about it. Whitmore was already combating her students' growing comfort with search engines (at home and school) by teaching her fifth and sixth graders webpage-evaluation skills, discussing cookies and other privacy issues, advocating website preselection, and promoting noncommercial subject directories such as KidsClick to her fellow teachers. KidsClick (www.kidsclick.org) was established by media specialists in New Jersey and was based on the nonprofit premise that "providing an objective information service for children is not compatible with simultaneously targeting them with marketing." A group of K–12 media specialists, rather than staff at Yahoo! or AOL@School, handpick KidClick's web selections according to their educational utility and value. Whitmore believed that such efforts were crucial to the future of the web as an educational tool; for her, media specialists and teachers, not commercial forces, were the ones who should be responsible for locating webpages and maintaining education-oriented subject gateways.

Whitmore felt so strongly that her students were too reliant on search engines—which in her view were overly commercial and a giant waste of time during internet lab sessions—that she had begun to create a noncommercial subject gateway on her own. One reason was to steer the school's students away from overly commercial sites and toward what she considered high-quality, credible sites. Another, and in her view perhaps a more important reason was to steer her students toward *existing library resources* in addition to her selection of "quality" web links. Using her knowledge of mark record cataloging, Whitmore had figured out how to integrate active website links into Hillup's online library catalog and was self-sufficiently building her own directory, selecting sites according to the same criteria she used for other library sources. Her evolving online directory allowed students to locate the websites she selected through the same search terms they would use to find books, thereby merging *all* library resources—books, CD-ROMs, videos, internet sites—into one coherent database.

A main worry for Whitmore was that students, in her experience, increasingly rely on websites, not books, for all their information. "I really feel with the way the Internet is going as a resource that we have an obligation to do this," she said. "The beauty of it is that it's within the library catalog. What we need to do is broaden kids' scope in terms of looking at the way kids do research." She got the idea from the Follett Software product WebPath Express. WebPath Express is essentially a card-catalog software program with links to a [now defunct] commercial educational subject directory called Webivor. Whitmore liked the concept behind the WebPath Express software—preselected and categorized web links that made up one aspect of a larger library catalog—but she was not impressed by Webivor's site listings or the price: about $1,000 for the initial yearlong subscription in 2001 and $700 for annual renewals. Instead of subscribing, she merged her own preselected websites into the school's established online database. In doing so, Whitmore was attempting to contain the web within the structure of the library catalog, where it was beyond commercial control. Whitmore even had plans to make her online library resource the internet portal page for Hillup Elementary, rather than the commercial portal used at the time of the study: Yahooligans!.

Whitmore's cataloging efforts, which really were in the fledgling stages and not yet utilized by other teachers at Hillup, were nevertheless inspiring. Most of the educators in this study considered the web to be an exciting and already evolved resource. In their view, it simply kept growing bigger; they did not feel it was evolv*ing* into a complicated environment that largely benefited commercial interests. Moreover, search engines seemed to work just fine for their purposes. Whitmore, and to a lesser extent, Stroh, Lowell, and LeRouge, addressed the web as a more complicated environment and worked hard to give their students adequate skills in negotiating this environment.

Considering all these efforts to make sense of the web and integrate web content into school assignments—preselection, power searching, webpage evaluation, and various (albeit spotty) discussions on internet privacy and profiling—I now turn to these educators' students. How were students determining what information to use for their research, or addressing the web overall? To what extent were the students heeding their teachers' suggestions? What were their teachers up against?

STUDENTS: SEARCH AND (NOT) FIND

The students I got to know during my school investigation had all been through some form of webpage-evaluation instruction. The 18 sixth graders in Melanie DeBower's class had received an orientation from the school's very competent media specialist, Jill Whitmore. The 19 eighth graders—18 boys and only 1 girl—in Jack Stroh and Miriam Lowell's Electronic Technology and Learning class had gone through the intense internet unit, although it had been a full month since they had discussed webpage-evaluation techniques or completed their Boolean tutorial and other domain activities. The thirty-six 11th and 12th graders in Steve LeRouge's two Comprehension and Perception English classes (18 in both classes) had just been through a lively session on webpage critique with LeRouge, discussing Boolean operators and carefully demonstrating how to apply the evaluation criteria to an untrustworthy webpage. They had also been introduced to Boolean searching techniques during their freshman orientation at the school library. At the time I observed all these students surfing the web, they were locating information for class research projects. These were smart and friendly students, and I enjoyed talking with them. They taught me a lot about what it's like being a student, working on a research project, and relying on search engines almost exclusively to locate materials online.

All the students I observed were searching for factual online information during numerous lab research sessions. Only a few (in LeRouge's advanced-level English classes) were using other library resources (e.g., magazine databases, books) beyond the web for their projects, and all agreed that they typically use the web alone for nearly all their school-related research projects. Every student was using a commercial search engine. Professing to be extremely comfortable typing in keywords and sorting through search results, these students—even the sixth graders—were gathering information on a great variety of topics. The sixth graders searched for sites on wetland environmentalism and voting. The eighth graders searched for sites on science-related themes such as tectonic plates, volcanoes, and galaxies; literature-related themes such as Edgar Allan Poe and Hans Christian Andersen; and other topics such as basketball history. The high school students searched for sites on an even wider range of topics, including the Holocaust, UFOs, aviation, violence in sports, Ritalin, music censorship, the Ebola virus, Ecstacy, the 1920s, communism, and waste management. For the purposes of their projects (and in the context of the webpage-evaluation unit in which these projects were assigned), they had to use information that they felt was reliable and authentic. With the exception of the sixth graders, they also had to document their sources for their final project.

Students' favorite search engines were Yahoo!, AltaVista, and Excite! (these were especially popular among the sixth graders), Lycos, Search.com, Dogpile, Google, Ask Jeeves, Sherlock, and Goto (now called Overture). Rationale for picking a particular search engine varied depending upon a students' level of internet experience. For example, less experienced users tended to settle upon Yahoo! because they sensed it was the most popular and therefore the best ("I see it on TV a lot. My cousin uses it. My mom uses it. So I'm just going to use it"). One student liked Lycos because he was taken by the company's high-profile television advertising ("It first got me in by the dog [in the ad]. I have to admit I like the dog. And I went into it"). Other students picked the search engine they felt seemed the most "professional" (Lycos was described this way numerous times) or picked one that, such as Search.com, had an easy-to-type name. The most experienced user in this study—a junior high school student—routinely progressed through a range of search engines and gateways: He began with AltaVista because he felt it gave him the broadest scope and offered the most accessible website summaries; then he turned to

Yahoo! (the search engine, not the directory) because he felt it was a little more focused. Finally, he turned to an encyclopedia website such as Britannica.com or Encarta.com, to narrow his search even further.

This student was the only one who ever discussed using an educational subject gateway (although I never did see him use one). As I discovered, the common notion among students was that subject gateways were for babies—they were coddled environments that in no way represented "the whole web." Students clearly thought they would miss out on important information if they did not use search engines. They also didn't like them because they seemed to require more work. On a few occasions, students came across such sites (e.g., Britannica.com and the Lightspan Network) on their search engine result lists and linked to them quite accidentally; they immediately resented having to retype their keyword or deep-linking through a variety of subject headings. Ironically, these tools often supplied students with exactly the type of factual and simplified information that they were looking for, but as this was not directly evident, they quickly gave up and returned to the back-and-forth comfort of their search engine lists.

Both the junior high and high school students overwhelmingly spoke to the ease and convenience of search engine research. "Oh, I think it's a lot easier than having to go and find books and look through the books," one high school student, Ron, told me. "The way you can skim it on the computer, it doesn't take as long to find it. All you have to do is type in a few words and there it is. You've got people [*sic*] there." Not leaving one's seat had definite appeal in the hunt for factual information. Although a few high school students used the online magazine databases that the school library subscribed to, where they could find current articles on a range of topics, they were clearly more impressed with the immediacy, scope, and currency of search engine result lists, even if a search often produced an overwhelming number of hits. "I'm looking up basketball so I just type in *basketball* and I search for it," Jeremy, a junior high school student, told me as he searched his topic on AltaVista and instantly reaped nearly 4 million hits.

The length of these lists never seemed to matter to students, because they believed that the most relevant sites appeared at the top of the list. While some students carefully read website summaries before linking to a particular site and skipped around a search engine list, most systematically began at the top of the list and went down, disregarding some links that seemed obviously irrelevant, but opening up many of the webpage links as they came to them. Many students had their own benchmark stopping point at which they would desert a result list and try a new search term or combination of terms. Students rarely went beyond the first three pages of a search engine list. "I usually just view the first page," Ty, a high school student, said. "I don't go on. If it says you can go to the next ten sites, I just stay with the first page." Another student, Lamont, told me, "[I stop] if I don't see anything on the first page. They get less relevant as you keep on going farther, so I'll just go one or two pages." In general, the students I talked to had faith that the search engines they used would give them good results within the first few pages of a list—if not the best, most thorough, and most current information of any available library resource. "I usually trust all of them [search engines]," Jeremy said. "I don't usually *not* trust anything. I don't usually come up with anything that is bad [i.e., pornographic, not trustworthy] or anything."

Interestingly, students did not try to power search with Boolean operators. When I asked them what they did when they got a list of more than 50,000 search engine results (which was typical), I would get answers such as "If there's a ton [of hits], I try to narrow it down by using 'ands' and 'ors' and all that kind of stuff," or "You kind of put quotation marks around the thing you mainly want, and that should cut it down," indicating that they did indeed remember certain elements of the Boolean terminology that they had learned in class. However, after many sessions observing these students using search engines, I saw no evidence that they ever used their advanced power-searching skills. Most often they typed in one word related to their research topic, like *basketball* or *volcanoes,* and reaped hits often numbering in the millions. One girl researching stars and galaxies on Yahoo! typed in *stars* and yielded about 23 million hits, including webpages for Star Trek, Star Wars, and male porn stars. She may have remembered power-searching techniques, but in practice she didn't use them, and instead resorted back to her more familiar habit of typing in a singular search term and instantly getting thousands of results.

Webpage Evaluation: Why Bother?

I also didn't see any effort to evaluate the webpages the students visited and used for their projects. From my just talking to students, it seemed to me that some of the webpage-evaluation guidelines had penetrated some of their thinking. I asked both junior high and high school students, for example, what they defined as a good website for their research, and a number of high school students echoed LeRouge in prioritizing objectivity: "I think a good webpage is like, how they explain both sides of the conflict, like for or against or whatever. And then they'll have like facts about it and stuff," Ted, a 12th grader, said. Similarly, Dina, an 11th grader, identified sites that were "not all gunked up by opinions and that kind of stuff." Other high school students cited author credibility as their high standard for a "good" webpage. "If it's quoted by like, people that you know, that are like reliable sources," Lamont said, "then I'll actually use it." Jess also noted the importance of contact information on a website, and whether or not an author was a known name rather than just some individual. For these students, truth and credibility seemed important to them when they spoke to me. But when I inquired a little further—"Do you actually go out of your way to determine whether a site is reliable?"—they said they did not, unless they were required to do so in class.

Furthermore, some students were applying their own method for determining author credibility that had nothing to do with Stroh's, Lowell's, or LeRouge's teachings. "If it's got information on it, I'll go for it, as long as two pages match up," Matt, an eighth grader, said. "I like to see if two pages match up. Like if I have one page with this information and another page with this information, if both of them have basically the same information." Two other students, one in junior high and one in high school, also said basically the same thing in completely separate interviews: "You know it's true if more than one guy agrees, or if more than one person agrees on it." It thus became evident throughout my observations that while teachers had rather painstakingly laid out particular strategies for searching the web and evaluating web content, their students were more interested in shortcuts. Moreover, the evaluative shortcuts used most often were ones that were even less connected to their teachers' lessons: speed and flashy design.

The Need for Speed

The drive to find web content (no matter what kind) as fast as possible was prevalent in all grades. As I observed sixth-grade students use search engines to locate images and facts for a unit on wetlands in Melanie DeBower's class, I found their approach to web material, which they were busily importing into a Hyperstudio stack, was akin to cutting out words and pictures from a magazine and gluing them onto posterboard. Student pairs moved quickly through the web, locating pictures of herons and alligators, or sentences relating to the wetland environment they were investigating, and slapping them onto a hypercard. Speed was such an issue that some students, thinking they could find a page faster than their partners, often grabbed the computer mouse from the other student. These students' single-minded mission to locate applicable photos and text had a consequence. They did not make distinctions about the kind of pages they were on, be it the Environmental Protection Agency site or a commercial tour guide site for the Everglades. Students treated the web as a stockpile of information at their complete disposal, and the faster they could find the information to complete their assignment, the better.

This emphasis on speed continued in the junior high and high school grades; students were in too much of a rush to care about the site-evaluation criteria they learned. For eighth grader Kevin, a good site was one that had "the information that you want and that you need." For eighth grader Bryan, "if it's got information on it, I'll go to it." Once again, their task—finding photos and short descriptive sentences quickly—allowed them to treat the web as a neutral space and webpage data as information for their taking, regardless of where it came from and what context it was framed in. As such, webpage domains were irrelevant to these students; websites were merely a huge collection of words, facts, and pictures that needed to be located (as quickly as possible) and assembled for academic purposes. "I just kind of go where the information is," Liz, who was searching for factual information on aviation, told me, even though she had sat through LeRouge's class period on webpage evaluation and had completed an assignment on webpage credibility. "I don't really care where it comes from."

In their quest for speed, students simply assigned credibility to websites that were the best organized and easiest to move around in. "I don't like the [webpages] where you have to keep clicking and clicking to get to it," Dina, an 11th grader, told me as she searched for online information on 1920s culture (indeed, students' distaste for deep linking explained exactly why they had such disdain for subject gateways). A well-organized site was more "professional" and was thus more credible. As eighth grader Jeremy told me, "If it's not well organized, I usually get out if it." Even a well-organized site was intolerable, though, if the information was too nuanced or required too much reading. "Some other sites I've looked at kinda beat around the bush before it gets to the main point," a high school student wrote in her webpage-evaluation critique. "This site tells me info right from the start."

Students looked for "short and sweet" information—the more succinct the information, the speedier it was to read and assess. Their favorite sites, accordingly, had all the information they needed laid out on the first (home) page. Corporate press releases often satisfied this need, as did short academic articles often connected to university course syllabi. The students I observed habitually steered away from webpages with "too much information" and constantly turned to pages with the most user-friendly, simplified content for their research projects. For Nick, a webpage with an extended paragraph already had too much information and was not worth reading. In this vein, students demanded a lot of pictures to supplement the short and sweet information they were looking for. A good page, then, was also one with lots of pictures.

Although high school students curdled at personal pages and websites created by the K–12 community ("that's a kindergarten page!"), the junior high students constantly relied on these sites for their information, even when Stroh and Lowell advised them not to. As eighth grader Jeremy remarked, "I always like [personal pages] almost better because, I don't know, I feel like I get more information." Personal and school-related pages were helpful to him because they offered the most direct information with the least amount of deep-linking and minimal commercial distractions. They are usually compact, don't take long to load up, and often have a clear purpose, devoted to a single topic. "There was this homepage I was at yesterday," Ashley, an eighth grader, commented while surfing. "It was some girl's homepage, and it told all about stars. . . . it was kind of cool. . . . it was a nice page." Ashley ended up using the page for her final project. In fact, most of the eighth graders had located personal or K–12 pages and used them as credible sources for their final webpage design project. The junior high school students' reliance on personal pages was the only significant difference between the grade levels in evaluating sites.

The Love of Design

A second shortcut that students tended to use to determine a website's credibility was the site's design—especially how appealing, fun, and cool the site looked. A professional-looking design, as mentioned above, made the webpage seem more credible, but students were also drawn to "flashy art" and pictures, which they often felt was a positive feature of any website. For example, Jeremy, an eighth grader, found two webpages that contained the exact same information; one version was in plain text format and the other was designed with a thick white font against a wood-paneling-type background. "See, I would probably like this site better just because of the [wood panel] background," he told me, clearly impressed by the page. Jeremy ended up using this page—created by the Kansas Heritage Center for Family and Local History—for his research. The logic was apparently this: If a webpage author had put a little more time into the choice of a background, then he or she had put more time into providing legitimate information.

When students ventured a critique of websites (as came up a few times in the eighth grader's Domain Search Activity papers), they most often based their critique on the site's design, not the information on the page. In observing the nonprofit Internet Public Library website (created and sponsored by the University of Michigan's School of Information) and its extensive and comprehensive newspaper database for his Domain Search Activity paper (a site his teachers, Stroh and Lowell, required him to visit), eighth grader Mark complained that the site was too boring to be worthwhile. "I have no pictures or anything interesting to look at," he said. "They don't even have a neat background." Correspondingly, Mark described a K–12 school site on mummies as incredibly appealing, but it was the site's design, not its validity or coverage, that appealed to him. In his paper for the project, he wrote:

> I like how this page is set up. They have a lot of buttons to
> pick from and they are neat little pictures. They also have a
> little info about what time period they cyber mummy was
> baried [sic]. They also have some kind of hieroglyphic things
> at the bottom. They also have a little sun thing in the back-
> ground that looks really cool.

Carla, an 11th grader who was doing research on tattoos, also defined a quality site in terms of the way it was set up, saying, "Like when you first look at it, if it attracts me, if it's colorful to look at . . . if it's not, I move on." For many students, appealing graphic components often included games or shopping opportunities. They commented on the ability to buy things—on a museum page, for example—as being a positive element of the page. "It's cool because you can win skateboards and other cool skateboarding stuff," one eighth-grade student wrote for a Domain Search Activity description. "You can buy new boards and shoes . . . the pictures in the gallery are cool too. In all, it's a really good site."

Hating Web Ads: Being Caught in the Mousetrap

Many students found online advertising "fun" and "catchy." Others, like their teachers, felt impervious to it. "It doesn't bother me" and "it's everywhere" were typical responses. Three sixth graders I observed seemed fully capable of ignoring a banner ad for the AT&T WorldNet Service that featured an animated red car dropping into the banner screen over and over again. But then again, maybe it just depended on the ad. "Hey!" the middle boy called out to his friends on either side of him as a new ad appeared on the screen, "I can get a newsletter sent to my home. Look up here!"

Other students, all eighth graders, admitted to clicking on certain ads if they seemed interesting. Some clicked on ads quite by accident. Kevin, an eighth grader, for example, had told me that ads were not distracting to him, but he repeatedly found himself on commercial sites thick with advertising messages and shopping appeals, all of which slowed down his hunt for useful information. Kevin often clicked quickly without reading the link tag and frequently opened up ads (pop-up screens and entire webpages) by accident. On one occasion he was caught in an advertising loop after he accidentally opened the pop-up ad for "BuyBuddy.com—register to WIN!!" on a magazine site called Ecoworld (www.ecoworld.com). Kevin had been "mousetrapped," and he needed my help to get out of it. Likewise, Ashley became immersed in GeoCities, a webpage-building service owned by Yahoo! (geocities.yahoo.com), which she had actually clicked on from a commercial science-information site on Jupiter (planetscapes.com).

Consequently, even if they were successful at ignoring the bulk of the advertising, many students got caught by it, and they often complained about the nuisance of closing box after box of advertising in order to finally access the desired webpage—another indicator of their passion for speed. As these two high school students observed:

> A lot of times like an ad will come up and you'll click out of it, and then like you say you'll click on something else on that page, but then if you have like the backbone, then [the ad] will come up again. And that gets annoying. Like sometimes if they pop up, like eight or nine will pop up, and if you click out of those, more will pop up, so . . . And they do get annoying, but . . . (Wes, 18)
>
> Oh, I'm always clicking commercials *off*. They are so annoying. And they come up every single time you click on a different page, like, if I just click here, a commercial will come up. And I hate the ones that just pop up, and I can't get rid of them. So they're very annoying . . . I hate the ones that, the pornographic sites that come up . . . you're searching for a topic and that stuff comes up and "I don't want to see that," that's gross. (Danielle, 17)

If students were resigned to the presence of online ads, they also had to proactively take the time to click off online advertisements, a process that regularly impeded their fact-finding efforts. As one eighth-grade student, Ed, summarized, "I try to stay away from them, 'cause when you're doing work, you look at that and it might be interesting, and then you don't go back."

Loving Web Ads:
Shocking the Monkey and Climbing the Banana Tree

I talked to a significant number of students at both the junior high and high school level who were drawn to games and contests and freely disclosed to such websites their contact information, as well as various consumer and lifestyle preferences, without a second thought. Lamont (11th grade), regularly played contests if they took 2 minutes or less to play; Bryan (8th grade) acknowledged that "they pull you in because it's fun. I like doing fun stuff like that"; Jeremy (8th grade) filled out contests to win magazines; and Mandy (high school) had given her email address out so many times she had become inundated by spam:

> *Mandy*: Mostly it's like the gross porn crap, that if you click
> on it they are like . . . [sarcastic] that's OK. But like maga-
> zines, *Alloy*, I get like something from them all the time
> and I don't know why. And I get, I get spammed on one
> of my emails, it's like the "tree loot" thing.
> *BF*: The tree loot thing?
> *Mandy*: Yeah. It was on a banner and it said "hit the monkey
> and win $20."

Tree Loot, as I would learn, was one of the most popular game-adver-
tisements on the internet at the time I conducted this study. The company responsible for Tree Loot, Virtumundo, places banner ads all over
the internet inviting users to "Shock the Monkey and WIN" as the company's mascot, a geeky-looking cartoon monkey, bounces back and
forth across the screen. Users who click on the ad are then introduced
to the Tree Loot game, in which they click on a tree and try to uncover
"banana bucks"—up to $25,000 if they're willing to put in the time;
banana bucks come in $20 increments. Banana bucks can be redeemed
for real prizes (e.g., digital watches, stuffed monkeys) as long as visi-
tors fill out a long survey that identifies their address, educational
background, income, hobbies, and 70 other "interest variables."

As I found from observing and videotaping students doing online
research for their school projects, the Tree Loot banner ad was one of
the most prevalent ones that appeared on their screens. The Tree Loot
website (www.virtumundo.com) earned a spot on the "top 50 most
visited Websites" list provided by Media Metrix in 2000 and happened
to be advertised (sometimes more than once) during 4 of the 21 student searches I observed, reaching nearly a fifth of my student participants. Indeed, most of the students I talked to about Shock the
Monkey/Tree Loot had heard of it. Bryan was researching Hans
Christian Andersen when he came across the Tree Loot game:

> *Bryan*: Oh, I *love* this stuff! (He clicks on ad . . . and it says,
> "You won $20!"). What it is, is, if you shock the monkey
> you get $20, you just have to punch the monkey, and
> catch the monkey, and kill the Pikachu, and stuff like that.
> *BF*: Really? What's it for?
> *Bryan*: It's for, I think it's for Bananatree, let me check (types
> in Bananatree . . .) I *love* going to these. I've got, they still
> owe me like a lot of money!

BF: So what is Bananatree.com?

Bryan: It's like a site where you get to go and you have to guess where money is, and they have like thousands of dollars but you can only go on their site and spend it, and you can get $20 off or something. It costs like $2 banana bucks or something, and you can't get one thing twice. Oh, man, is that how you spell banana?

BF: Yes.

Bryan: Well I want to get here . . . they said I won 20 bucks, how do I get there? That's agitating!

BF: So it's banana money, it's not real money?

Bryan: Yeah, it's just . . .

BF: And then what do you do with the money?

Bryan: You go onto the internet and, oh, there it is . . . Tree Loot! This is *Tree Loot*, duh! Oh, man, now they're doing the one-man shock, they did this last week. How you do this, you go on and you get money. Here's how it starts, let me show you (clicks on the tree). You have that, and there's this huge tree, and if you guess where the monkeys are, and then . . . they put that there just to fool you (some symbol on the tree). . . . And you put in your name and you have to sign up and everything.

BF: So you put in your name and your email and everything?

Bryan: Yeah, and then they send you stuff, and my email is so . . . My email can only be accessed at home, and it is *so long*.

BF: So what kind of things do they send you?

Bryan: They send you like, "we've got a new thing this week and . . . you know . . . "

BF: Do you have a sense that they've passed your email on to other companies?

Bryan: Sometimes I do, but if I ever get anything from somebody I basically don't know, I've learned from basic Preferences not to open it. So . . . I've opened stuff I don't want.

BF: Have you actually ever won anything online?

Bryan: Yeah, but they never emailed me about it.

BF: Oh really?

Bryan: Yeah, I won a gift certificate for Blockbuster.

BF: Oh no!

Bryan: Yeah, I know, it was for a couple of free movies, and I wouldn't have to buy them, and video games, and I like video games, I like to play video games.

BF: You won a video game? So how often do you go on this Tree Loot?

Bryan: If I have any extra time I always go on here, it's just fun.

BF: How did you find it in the first place, just from the advertisements on top?

Bryan: Like they give you a shot at punching a monkey if you go to their sponsors. They do stuff like that. If you punch the monkey you can put $75 in your pocket.

BF: So they have ads all over the place then.

Bryan: Yeah, then they get you into it, and you just click . . . you just keep it . . . See then, it says, "Hey friend, welcome back." Did I win anything? No!

BF: So what do you think about all this stuff on the screen that's beyond the information that you're trying to look for? Do you tend to click on stuff that moves just because it's fun, or you're curious?

Bryan: Sometimes, if it looks fun I probably would. I'm not one to click on something like that (he points to a "Casino" banner ad).

BF: So that looks kind of dumb.

Bryan: Yeah, kinda! This looks fun but still I can't do it because I'm not exactly the rightful age to be on that site. I've been there before and you have to be 18 and a credit card holder.

BF: Have you ever bought anything online?

Bryan: I have coaxed my mother to help me so I can get something else in return but she keeps saying no because you always need a credit card. (Bryan continues to play the Tree Loot game).

Bryan: I know I've got $5 in here somewhere . . .

BF: So you can keep coming back and trying?

Bryan: Yeah, you can try the whole day, and they just give you tips and you win money, and see, I'll show you, it'll give you a list of stuff and then it'll say, "We're going to email you tomorrow about it . . . " That's basically it. That's how they pull you in like this!

Of course, Bryan was avidly playing Tree Loot as he talked to me. Perhaps because of my questions and his zeal to explain the game to me, Bryan may not have played at such length during class time—the other three students I observed actually ignored the invitation to shock the monkey as they conducted their online research. Clearly, however, the ad and the game were enticing for Bryan, who played games like Tree Loot and Kill the Pikachu regularly. Interestingly, Bryan seemed to be quite aware that playing games and entering contests led to email spam and that various strategies existed to "pull you in." Even so, he was clearly taken by the promise of real prizes, and he played games whenever he had the chance. He was not bothered by "long" email lists with lots of spam; perhaps it made him feel important. When it came to researching Hans Christian Andersen or playing Tree Loot, one thing is for sure: Bryan was much more focused when he was playing games.

Searching on the Commercial Highway

The advertisements and gaming opportunities were certainly distracting to students, but many were capable of ignoring them. Bryan was an extreme case. However, perhaps the most disconcerting were the kinds of sites that students selected on their search result lists. As I have established, students searching often generated lists with thousands and even millions of search engine results. They didn't tend to use Boolean operators to narrow down the list and they had faith that the most relevant search engine results appeared at the very top of the list—on the first or second page. In their view, there was little point in narrowing down the list if the most relevant sites appeared at the top anyway. What wasn't obvious to them was that for most of their searches, multiple links led to the same sites, bulking up the first few pages with a remarkable amount of redundancy. For example, Wes (11th grade), who was conducting research on Ebola, found that most of the relevant-sounding pages he opened led to the same set of out-of-date documents published by the World Health Organization. Jess was having a similar experience in his research on the Nuremburg trials. "It's all like the same thing," he said. "Like it's a different person who put it on the web, but it's like the same articles, like it's written by the same guy and they just copied it." These remarks were made only after I began asking students about link redundancies. Most of the time, I saw lots of repetition and no significant reaction among students.

Another thing that wasn't obvious to students doing online research was that most of the sites at the front end of their search result lists linked to commercial services—the result of search engines' increasingly aggressive pay-for-placement and paid-inclusion strategies. Of course, different topics influenced the number of commercial hits that students got at the top of search engine lists, and students searched the web under a wide range of topics. If they were investigating waste management or communism, for example, they received fewer commercial hits than they would have had for basketball history or tattoos. All the same, students were inundated by commercial sites. Of course, there are numerous commercial sites—for example, HowStuffWorks, the Discovery Network, Amazon.com—that do offer tremendous topical information. The ones that inundated students' online research, however, wasted their time. Alex, who was searching for volcanoes, waded through websites on hotels, movies, volcano tours, and science superstores (he had typed in *volcanoes*). Mick, who was investigating Edgar Allan Poe on the search engine Dogpile, had to read through 16 link summaries to commercial sites (e.g., Papers for Edgar Allan Poe for sale!; Find Edgar Allan Poe Items on ebay, Edgar Allan Poe Books at Barnes and Noble) before he came to a page that gave relevant historical information about the author. Kevin, who was searching for information on ocean life, was lost in a maze of shopping pages. Instead of carefully reading the summaries beneath the websites, Kevin clicked on "Great Ocean Decorations," which led him to "Nautical Seasons: Enter Our Store," which led him to "Barnacle Kove—We ship to your door," and then another shopping site. At one point Kevin said with resignation, "Every site you go to almost is trying to sell you something." Will (11th grade) was searching for Ebola and came across site after site by the same author, Dr. Len Horowitz, from Tufts University, marketing his books on the topic. Similarly, Seb (eighth grade) was doing research on the rock cycle and came to a site with pictures of rocks and minerals aligned on a grid. "This is a fossil site," he said, reading on. "I thought I just could get some pictures. But it's . . . just selling stuff. I thought it had more information on it." When I asked him if a lot of the sites he visited were trying to sell stuff, Seb echoed Kevin, saying, "Everybody is trying to sell you something."

In addition to clicking on the many commercial sites within a given search result list, students regularly clicked on the "sponsored links" featured in all search engine result pages. The three or four sponsored links before the actual search results begin has become a standard element of commercial search engines. They are paying sites and further add to the commercialism on the web, while crowding out educational and nonprofit sites, which likely aren't paying for placement. Most search engines strategically don't distinguish between the sponsored links at the top of the list and the rest of the search engine results. However, at the time this study was conducted, the search engine AltaVista subtly differentiated its sponsored links from the rest of the search results by color—green for sponsored, blue for search results. Despite the distinction, I observed students trying out the sponsored links, believing that any site listed at the top of a search engine list was worthwhile. Even those who fully recognized that these links were sponsored selected them regularly. For example, as eighth grader Jeremy searched on AltaVista we had the following conversation:

> *Jeremy*: These green ones are sponsored ones.
> *BF*: So these are sponsored listings, and they come first?
> *Jeremy*: Yeah.
> *BF*: So you don't really go to those?
> *Jeremy*: Well I try them out, but usually they're not very good.
> *BF*: Really?
> *Jeremy*: Yeah.

By 2001 AltaVista used an even more deceptive strategy to separate the sponsored links from the other search results. The company replaced both the blue and green colors with light gray and left a fine line—three indistinguishable dots—between sponsored and nonsponsored sites. If students were already taken in by sponsored links clearly designated by a different color, they would likely be taken in even more by sponsored links with barely any distinction at all.

As I watched students conduct their online research during class time, I observed many futile and frustrating searches for information. Even though the students I interviewed remained committed to doing online research—nearly every student I talked to relied almost completely on the web for their research information—a small number admitted that libraries and magazine databases were serving them better, at least for the subject they were currently investigating. For these students, the web was no library, or information highway, with all the information they needed at their fingertips. As Nick, who was

doing research on sports violence and was completely dissatisfied
with his searching experience, summarized:

> I don't know, it reads just like an advertisement for things.
> It's hard to find information for you to really use. That you
> know is true. . . . It just looks like one big advertisement to
> me. I try to spend as little time as possible on it.

From Nick's point of view, the web was a commercial highway complete with billboards, strip malls, information potholes, and the same
big chain stores over and over again.

Even so, most students did not experience Nick's frustration; they
were more comfortable wading through ads, shopping pages, redun-
dant sites, and corporate public relations than they were wading
through more comprehensive texts on particular topics. They were
sure they were using the most comprehensive information resource
available and were pleased that they didn't even have to get up from
their chairs.

CHAPTER 6

Visions of a Better Internet

If the monopolization of Internet navigation by commercial interests is allowed to continue, the next millennium may see the democratizing aspects of the medium decline to the point where it will be of little use, except for marketing communications.

—Jan Samoriski, 2000

The most important thing about the World Wide Web is that it is universal. By exploring this idea along its many axes we find a framework for considering its history, its role today, and guidance for future developments.

—Tim Berners-Lee, 2002

The internet is different from all other communications and educational media. Of course it's different in that it's a platform on which all media converge; it has unlimited space; creating and distributing web content is relatively easy (after the initial wiring and computer expenses are outlaid); and it's a global medium—extending its reach to voices and people around the world. But the internet is also different in that, unlike for any medium before it, the government backed it as a school technology. Never before had any educational medium been so fervently pushed and so richly financed, allowing it to be widely adopted in schools and businesses, and homes as well.

But with all the expense to get schools wired, and the expanded rhetoric about the information superhighway, where's the educational content? One could say it's everywhere and nowhere. Students think it's everywhere, relying on the web for the bulk of their school research and social activities—their research projects are based on the content they find online. And why not? They are comfortable with this medium. They reap millions of search engine hits. They have their own searching shortcuts in place. Believing that search engines offer them a research utopia at their fingertips, students expect search engines to deliver information as promised: quickly and effortlessly, no matter who the content provider is. Influenced by flashy, appealing design elements, students play into advertisers' dreams. They determine webpage credibility by the most eye-catching design, not the most comprehensive content. Consequently, they overlook credible— yet plainly designed—sites such as the Internet Public Library, which has one of the most comprehensive newspaper, magazine, and serial databases available online. They skip over ibiblio, which requires that they deep link into the website's rich archives. As such, students are adopting a consumer, rather than an intellectual, mindset in their approach to information. Although the packaging has no appreciable relationship to the content, students mistakenly perceive that it does. In other words, critical thinking goes out the window.

This is not necessarily students' fault, or the fault of their teachers. The problem is that delivering organized academic content to students—consolidating useful online information for the purposes of education alone—has not been a national priority. Indeed, educators in Walnutville and nationwide have a dilemma: Reminiscent of the adage that warns, "Don't bite the hand that feeds you," it's difficult to critique what you've asked for—or what you've been given. Educators feel obliged to focus on the positive aspects of the web—its power, its many outstanding websites, its richness—not its advertisements, its marketing schemes, its deceptive navigational tools, its commercial clutter, and the relative lack of website coordination for the purposes of education. The status quo of commercial domination of media technology seems just fine from the U.S. government's point of view—it has been since the radio era. Meanwhile, educators publish meek how-to guides to "good" websites, but explicitly avoid concerted discussions about where online content is going, how this content should be harnessed for schools, and who should do the harnessing. To begin such a wholesale critique of the web and its commercial evolution requires a great deal of resolve. It means that we have to question the economic, political, and social fabric of American life. To demand better-organized online content requires even more resolve. It means calling for a national educational portal, competing with commercial vendors, and insisting on public funding. None of this is easy, but this is what we have to do.

STEPS TO TAKE

Despite many educators' expressed annoyance and frustration with the increasing for-profit imperatives of the internet, it remains to be seen if educators have any solutions to the internet's troubling trajectory. I am proposing action in two areas that may help harness the internet for educational purposes, even as the commercial highway becomes more pronounced. The first area concerns web criticism, and the second concerns web content.

Web Criticism

As illustrated by the Walnutville case study, teachers already have methods available for critiquing webpages. But to understand the entire internet from a critical perspective, the critique needs to be more expansive. This means finding ways to help teachers step from a critical reading of individual webpages to a *critical literacy* approach to the entire internet. Cervetti, Pardales, and Damico (2001) make helpful distinctions between critical reading practices and critical literacy: Critical reading is all about figuring out the "correct" meaning of a text—be it a letter, a book, a TV sitcom, or hip-hop lyrics. For example, a student reads a Shakespeare play in English class and tries to understand what Shakespeare *really* meant. In examining a text's truthfulness and reliability, critical readers can then evaluate its function in society. This is the way webpage evaluation is currently taught in most classrooms—students are generally asked to decipher which webpages offer the most valid or "quality" factual data, and then they use the "best" data to write objective, fact-based reports on a single issue.

As Cervetti and colleagues (2001) explain, critical literacy acquaints students with the social, historical, political, and economic dimensions of all texts. Far beyond trying to decode the true intentions of a text's author, critical literacy teachers ask questions about what the text is and can be for others, how it was written and organized, under what conditions it was written and organized, and for what purposes. Furthermore, students reading the texts are encouraged to ask what perspective the texts advance and whether these perspectives should be accepted:

> Learners begin to reflect critically on the nature of literacy and literacies as social practices. Once they recognize that texts are representa-

tions of reality and that these representations are social constructions, they have a greater opportunity to take a more powerful position with respect to these texts—to reject them or reconstruct them in ways that are more consistent with their own experiences in the world. (Cervetti et al., 2001, p. 3)

In a critical literacy approach to discussing online content, questions would be more in the realm of how and why websites are constructed, how many target audiences can be identified, what the design genres of a particular site are, what persuasive strategies are in place to keep users engaged with a particular webpage (see C. Luke, 2000, p. 427), and what information *isn't* present and why (see Burbules & Callister, 2000; Frechette, 2002). In Burbules and Callister's words, a critically literate assessment of internet material uses discussions about misinformation, malinformation, messed-up information, and mostly useless information to highlight and reflect upon the procedures and criteria by which people identify information as "mis," "mal," "messed-up," or "mostly useless" (p. 117). Rather than being concerned with pure evaluation (good vs. bad), it places all information on an ideological continuum.

High school teachers might apply critical literacy, for example, to a discussion of Johnny Appleseed—a popular character in U.S. elementary education. A search of his name on Google will deliver an abundance of sites—many targeting elementary (K–4) school teachers and students—that discuss Johnny Appleseed as a "folk hero." This is what I encountered on a June 2003 search of "Johnny Appleseed" on Google: The first hundred or so sites included promotional pages for the apple juice industry; teacher lesson-plan websites (both commercial and nonprofit); and sites for organizations, nature trails, festivals, ecology clubs, and the like that simply contained the name Johnny Appleseed. These sites typically described John Chapman (his real name) in limited terms—terms very similar to those of the 1948 Disney cartoon *The Legend of Johnny Appleseed*: He was a kind and generous man, but a bit of a loner, who planted apple trees, carried a Bible, went barefoot, and wore a pot on his head as a hat; he is famous for delivering apples to settlers by planting thousands of apple trees. These website descriptions (the kind of "factual" information students are often told to look for on the web) were most often accompanied by a cartoon image of a smiling Johnny Appleseed wearing a pot and eating an apple. Many of the sites also suggested a broad assortment of activities that teachers and students can do with apples: make apple pies, eat apples, eat or make applesauce, visit an apple orchard to pick (and eat) apples, and even invite a Johnny Appleseed look-alike to come to the classroom, hand out apples, and talk about Johnny Appleseed, the pioneer hero. All these sites appeared to be purely factual. They offered corroborating, objective-sounding information as well as contact information for the webpage creators. Some even posted web awards. One might conclude that these websites—the most popular Johnny Appleseed sites on the web, according to Google's search engine method—reveal the truth about Johnny Appleseed. But in fact, they are merely perpetuating a myth that was established early in the 20th century, long after John Chapman died in 1845 (or thereabouts).

To better understand the mythology of Johnny Appleseed, it is helpful to turn to a book, not an internet site, for a fuller sense of how this man became canonized in U.S. culture. The book is called *The Botany of Desire* (2001) and is written by Michael Pollan, who, through historical investigation, personal musings, and his own knowledge of botany, has put together a much more complicated picture of John Chapman than any of the above web sources. For this history, Pollan also turned to books and print articles—now-forgotten biographies written between 1870 and 1955—which described John Chapman as a savvy businessman who professed the Swedenborgian doctrine (a sort of mystical mixture of Christianity and Buddhism); an entertainer and news informer frequently invited into settlers' homes; a strange man who may have had a predilection for young children, especially girls; and—despite his burlap-sack clothing and bare feet—a wealthy man. But the most interesting thing about Johnny Appleseed has more to do with apples than the man himself. As Pollan explains:

> It was a single botanical fact about the seeds themselves that made me realize that his story had been lost, and probably on purpose. The fact, simply, is this: apples don't "come true" from seeds—that is, an apple tree grown from a seed will be a wildling bearing little resemblance to its parent. Anyone who wants edible apples plants grafted trees, for the fruit of seedling apples is almost always inedible—"sour enough," Thoreau once wrote, "to set a squirrel's teeth on edge and make a jay scream." Thoreau claimed to like the taste of such apples, but most of his countrymen judged them good for little but hard cider—and hard cider was the fate of most apples grown in America up until Prohibition. Apples were something people drank. The reason people in Brilliant [Ohio] wanted John Chapman to stay and plant a nursery was the same reason he would soon be welcome in every cabin in Ohio: Johnny Appleseed was bringing the gift of alcohol to the frontier. (p. 9)

The botanical reality of apples, then, quite effectively disassembles the myth of Johnny Appleseed as the bringer of sweet-tasting apples to the frontier. Since hard cider was considered more sanitary than water, even children drank it by the bucketfuls. People and children on the frontier, in other words, were largely drunk. As Pollan reveals, it wasn't until the temperance movement in the early 1900s (which would lead to Prohibition in the 1920s) that hard cider would cease to become a popular U.S. beverage. And it was this movement against hard cider that forced the apple industry to create a need for apple eating, not apple drinking. The ensuing public relations campaign would popularize the slogan An apple a day keeps the doctor away, associate the apple with good teachers and school in general, and retool Johnny Appleseed, the Swedenborgian missionary, into a Christian saint who delivered apples, not hard cider, to the frontier. Today, Johnny Appleseed is embraced as a child's hero and celebrated in elementary schools.

While never claiming that his historical investigations got him "that much closer to the *real* John Chapman" (p. 6), Michael Pollan has managed to integrate Johnny Appleseed into a much broader cycle of economic, social, and historical events. In understanding the many dimensions of this myth, students can become aware of how information exists on a spectrum; they can observe how each website is no longer a factual document but an example of a myth perpetuated. They can go back to their Google search result list and see how many pages play into the sanitized version of Johnny Appleseed, and they can look for alternative versions of this story. It shouldn't come as a big surprise that the very first site returned in my Google search was the Processed Apple Institute's (aka the apple juice industry's) promotional page (www.applejuice.org/johnnyappleseed.html), which tells the Disney version of the man and even writes (perhaps erroneously) that John Chapman's favorite book was the Bible. With their new perspective, students can see the error, but understand why that error exists. The world is a complex place and facts are malleable; understanding this malleability is the goal of critical literacy. Students investigate why and how certain information becomes status quo, and they learn to understand that some perspectives are marginalized in this process.

Critical literacy depends upon synthesizing a variety of voices and points of view. In this case, Michael Pollan's discussions can be placed in direct contrast to the many websites, but also books and films, that romanticize and simplify John Chapman's life. However, analyzing

Johnny Appleseed information on the internet can also be a critical lesson on the limitations of the web itself as an "all-encompassing" information superhighway. If students try to find online webpages that go *against* the folk-hero myth, as Michael Pollan's book does, they will have great difficulty. In 2003, only *one* website among hundreds of a Google search offered a different, more complex perspective of John Chapman. Created by Professor David R. Williams (aka Dr. Dave), who teaches in the English department at George Mason University, the site is marked by the infamous tilde, and might suggest to some students an opinionated personal page. Indeed, the site is opinionated. "Anyone interested in cider in America needs to know the true story of America's number one appleholic, the first American hippie and religious freak, Jonathan Chapman." What Williams has posted, however, is an amazing primary document: the scanned version of the very first article written about John Chapman, "Johnny Appleseed: A Pioneer Hero," which was published in *Harpers* magazine in 1871. This is one of the very documents Pollan refers to in his own book.

It is a testament to the internet's versatility that this seldom seen article, now in the public domain (meaning it is so old it isn't subject to copyright restrictions) is online. Williams' page, available at http://mason.gmu.edu/~drwillia/apple.html, is also a testament to the internet's commercialization: The page has become increasingly hard to find. In 2002 it was on the fifth page of a Google search. By 2003, Dr. Dave's website, although still online, was not even considered among the first 25 pages (I gave up looking for it). The marginalization of this website (and the overwhelming redundancy of other Johnny Appleseed information) can generate good discussions, one hopes, about the lack of depth and variety of web information available to a student using a search engine. In addition, the use of Michael Pollan's highly acclaimed *The Botany of Desire* (which was a bestseller in 2001) can beautifully reiterate the value and importance of books in the age of the internet. It seems clear that students' entire online research experience would change if they developed a knowledge base about a subject before they began hunting, via search engines, for information. This would help students to then make informed critical judgments about online material and help them be more critical, on the whole, of the internet as a research tool.

One could also apply critical literacy to broaden a discussion about controversial steroid supplements such as creatine (baseball slugger Mark McGuire's supplement of choice), or diet supplements such as ephedra. Designer drugs fascinate high school students and, according to Walnutville teacher Steve LeRouge, are frequent student research topics, at least in his class. The following critical literacy exercise on ephedra (developed by Scott Harmsen of the University of Northern Iowa) asks students to conduct an initial Google search on the substance. The search will, inevitably, yield page after page of commercial ventures that supply "facts" about ephedra's benefits (while simultaneously trying to sell the drug). Other pages will be more subtle, masked as the literature of research institutes or educational organizations while really attempting to change public opinion to the supplement industry's advantage. (A closer look at the "Ephedra Education Council," for example, re.. 's that it is backed by companies with a huge stake in the diet supplement trade.) Using webpage-evaluation strategies (e.g., Who is the author/sponsor? How objective is the information?), students would investigate a number of pages on their search result list. But for a critical literacy approach to this topic, evaluating these webpages would just be the initial step. Students would then attempt to find documents on as many sides of the issue as possible: the commercial vendors, the government regulators, the various medical organizations (such as the American Medical Association or the American Heart Association), and the regular people sharing personal experiences. Since commercial search engines stack websites in favor of commercial vendors (edging out other voices), students would need to investigate newspaper and magazine articles, books, library databases, blogs, government resources, and a range of subject directories as well. Students would then develop a range of opinions using all the information gathered.

Next, students would begin investigating why certain opinions have prominence over others. To do this, they would need to check out the way these supplements have been regulated by two key industries: the Food and Drug Administration (FDA) and the Federal Trade Commission (FTC). With a little bit of probing on the FDA's site (indeed, there is much to find online), they would be able to find information on the Dietary Supplement Health and Education Act (DSHEA). The act, which was passed in the mid-1990s, essentially allowed the FDA to stop regulating the supplement industry. As a result, there is little oversight on the industry; scientific testing is not required to test the safety of a dietary supplement. Because Congress required the FDA to look the other way, there is now an avalanche of untested diet pill products, many of which are advertised and promoted on the internet. After learning about the FDA's role in deregulation, students would then go to the FTC website, the organization in charge of regulating trade practices. Here they would learn that the FTC is also largely required to turn a blind eye to the marketing and selling practices of this burgeoning and unsafe dietary supplement trade. They would learn, for example, that while the FTC was "concerned" about the explosion of unsafe diet pills, they felt that "self-regulation" was the best solution and called upon (but did not require) media outlets to verify whether an advertisement was truthful or not before allowing it to be printed or broadcast (Harmsen, 2003).

In proceeding through these government websites, and then relating current regulatory practices to the information on their search result list, students can better understand how government policy influences the kind of information they can find about ephedra and other dietary supplements. They might want to investigate further into the lobbying efforts behind the DSHEA. They could look at newspaper and magazine articles at the time of the DSHEA decision and document the controversy about the act. They might also consider a historical investigation, looking at the deluge of unregulated patent medicines in the 1900s, such as Lydia Pinkham's Vegetable Compound, that led to the creation of the FDA in 1906, and the political and economic pressures that lead to its current meek status as a regulatory body.

This kind of critical literacy investigation brings students into a much larger and more complicated world of ideas. It takes their critique of an individual webpage far beyond its adherence to credibility criteria and helps students understand that ideas are filtered through an economic, political, and social framework. Furthermore, this kind of critical literacy allows them to explore areas of the web—such as government sites—that they would not necessarily reach through a search engine. It shows them that a few pages of one book, or the careful reading of a federal law, can be more valuable than a million websites in terms of figuring out how our world works.

Moreover, if the web is demystified as an all-encompassing information superhighway, we can begin to understand how it is not a neutral resource and how its commercialism impedes the medium's chances to become the educational medium it could be (see Robins & Webster, 1999). Critical literacy discussions about search engines, subject gateways, and the problem of paid placement would be valuable in the classroom (see A. Luke, 2000). Investigations into the heavyweight internet and media companies, such as Time Warner, Microsoft, and Yahoo!, and their vision of the medium's future, contrasted with other visions of the internet, would also be valuable. Explorations into the marketing tactics of such data-gathering companies as Doubleclick and Virtumundo, filtering services such as N2H2, and school portal services such as AOL@School would be worthwhile, especially if students read, compared, and discussed company privacy policies, press releases, and annual reports—all of which are available on the web. Lessons about the internet's history as the country's newest mass medium, especially in relation to preceding mass media, would help students place the internet in its proper context. Discussions about what role the web should have in education is also imperative to understanding the medium as a resource for information, ideas, and learning. Finally, as Robins and Webster (1999) suggest, we should extend the discussion beyond the technology. "We must be concerned to explore the limits of the technoculture in the name of values that are more important and worthwhile," they write. "Those values will be in part directed against the new technologies, but more importantly against the capitalist imperative that drives and shapes the new technology agenda" (p. 6). In sum, we're shortchanging students by not letting them in on the bigger picture.

Web-based assignments should change too, reflecting some of the explorations and discussions mentioned above. Assignments such as the one Ted Rockenbrodt developed for his Developing Nations class, which asked students to pose as businesspeople and search for solely consumer information, only affirm to students that the internet serves (and should serve) commercial purposes. Furthermore, research projects, which traditionally require students to assemble objective facts gathered from the web (with webpage-evaluation assignments worked in between), should change too. I think it's important to help students understand the nonneutrality of all texts and regard the web as a place for opinions, not objective information, a place where the best developed arguments, not the slickest packaging, should gain their approval. As Kapitzke (2001) recommends, students should be gathering a multitude of perspectives, rather than objective facts, and learning to synthesize these perspectives. With opinion-based assignments—assignments that require students to think interpretively rather than regurgitate facts—the tendency to plagiarize off the web would certainly decrease as well.

If educators still adhere to assigning traditional fact-based research projects, then they should at least discourage students from relying solely on web search engines for their research. Educators should ask students to read a wide range of resources and allow them enough time to carefully do this research (or condition students with research schedules). We should not allow students to exclude a whole history of established library holdings just because it's easier for them to type in a keyword. If solid research is about triangulation, we should go beyond asking students to triangulate between web sources (as a few students in my study instinctively did), and ask them to triangulate between a number of library media in addition to the web.

Web Content

Another step to take is to steer students away from commercial search engines and acclimate them to subject gateways, which rely on content editors to organize web information into subject categories. The Walnutville students preferred the ease and speed of search engines, but—in terms of results—liked subject gateways. Unfortunately, these experiences with subject gateways were more accidental than planned. For example, Walnutville students found Lightspan and Britannica.com (before they both became fee based in 2001) quite helpful in their online fact-finding missions. Even though they entered the sites from their search engine lists, and begrudgingly retyped their key words into the portal's database (so time consuming!), they remarked at how perfect the gateway selections were that they found.

At the moment, however, educational subject gateways are, like search engines, dominated by commercial enterprise. The "free" subject gateway/school portal AOL@School is overtaking both the commercial and noncommercial educational web portal scene, gaining endorsements from a coterie of governors and administrators who are mandating that AOL@School become the default platform on school computers across districts and even states. Because it's not producing any original content, AOL@School has the relatively easy task of linking to already established educational web resources—such as a PBS page on the Civil War—or drawing upon the links that other services (e.g., the Librarian's Index to the Internet, the Internet Public Library, and the National Science Digital Library) have been organizing for years. Again, it is the monied sites such as AOL@School and Yahooligans! that can build strong brands with widespread advertising/public relations campaigns, large design budgets, and an attractive assortment of related services such as email and interactive games.

As the radio industry overpowered and absorbed educational stations and turned radio into an advertising-based medium, commercial
subject gateways have a similar economic incentive to become *the* educational resource of choice, overwhelming nonprofit subject gateways
and becoming the accepted standard in school, advertising and all. Less
outrage over in-school commercialism today, as compared to the radio
era, and a nonchalant attitude toward online commercialism among
educators and students may very well smooth this process. Yet what
will prevent these huge companies from reconsidering their "commitment" to education and the future of their "public service" portals?

As parent company Time Warner continues to have financial difficulties—particularly in its AOL unit—the already limited
AOL@School content will likely deteriorate. Yahoo!'s own history of
reversing privacy terms is indicative of its obligation to the public
interest (Baird, 2002). As its Yahooligans! subsidiary successfully over-
whelms its nonprofit counterparts and gains more power as an all-
purpose search tool and K–12 gateway, the company may decide that
its educational mission is over. This is what happened to Microsoft's
ambitious online education endeavor, Microsoft.com/education,
which today is a rambling mess. Although the site still offers a paltry
collection of lesson plans, these are mostly ideas on how to use
Microsoft products. Disney's "Edu-station" venture is now a venue for
Disney "learning" paraphernalia (e.g., the *Aladdin Storybook*; Pooh's
Balloon Game for the classroom, a game about letter identification);
and Apple's Global Education Network has found a niche as a fee-
based online course service.

Today AOL@School, the leading commercial education portal,
spends most of its energy "partnering" with other commercial educational initiatives, all of which have vested interests in promoting their
narrow online offerings. Generally speaking, when educational
motives are supplanted with profit motives, the outcome is rarely in
the best interest of students. For these reasons, it's best to use, promote,
and fund the significant number of *nonprofit* online subject gateways
that currently exist to steer users to education-minded webpages and
otherwise elusive material related to specific fields or disciplines.

Librarian-created subject gateways

Both public and academic librarians have been at the forefront of the
webpage-sorting effort. Some initiatives have benefited from state spon-

sorship. The Michigan Electronic Library (MeL), for example, developed by librarians in 1992, was one of the first subject-based catalogs on the internet. KidsClick! was established within the Ramapo Catskill Library System in New Jersey. The site, which serves the K–12 community, is now maintained via the Colorado State Library. The Librarians Index to the Internet (lii) operates out of California's Public Library System and draws upon librarian contributors in California and Washington state. Other initiatives have developed out of large research universities. Perhaps the most well known of this genre is the Internet Scout Project (based at the University of Wisconsin) and the Internet Public Library (based at the University of Michigan's School of Information). Both projects serve the public library and K–12 communities. The Internet Public Library also works as a training ground for graduate students at the university, as well as a research tool for faculty.

Academic librarians are also heavily involved in broadly defined subject gateways that mainly serve the needs of higher education. INFOMINE is based at the University of California and relies upon librarian input from a number of other universities; the Gateway to Online Resources is affiliated with the University of Iowa; and InfoTree is affiliated with Ohio University. Indeed, there is a lot of redundancy, with academic librarians at all major research universities offering some sort of internal gateway to selected web resources. All these projects cover a vast selection of content categories (e.g., arts and humanities; business and economics; computers and internet), which are then divided into more specific subheads.

Meanwhile, the Online Computer Library Center (OCLC), the world's most prominent library cooperative (serving more than 40,000 libraries worldwide with cataloging services) has moved to integrate selected web links into its database. As such, users at an OCLC-affiliated library can find relevant academic websites while they search for books and other library holdings. This idea is very similar to what Hillup media specialist Jill Whitmore was attempting to do with her own elementary school catalog—including all academic resources, web and others, under the same cataloging system.

Finally, nearly every academic library at institutions of higher education, as well as many other museums and archives, are actively digitizing special collections and putting them online—all types of printed and written documents, as well as maps, photos, theses, journals, audio, film, and video. Unlike the subject gateway model, which features external links to webpages, these digital repositories are internally generated: scientific contributions from the University of Bologna, photo collections of the Boston Gas Company from Boston College, a collection of poems by British women from the University of California. New academic content is being generated by libraries, societies, and organizations by the hour.

Citizen-created subject gateways

While librarians and archivists are dedicated to the control and access of approved, "known" material, other noncommercial subject gateways eschew library knowledge and champion citizen and scholarly experts. The Open Directory Project, for example, is a grassroots, open source movement phenomenon. Volunteer citizens, not librarians, add webpages to the directory and edit subject headings. "Citizens can each organize a small portion of the web," the project's website reads, "and present it back to the rest of the population, culling out the bad and useless and keeping only the best content" ("About," 2003). The Open Directory's free and formidable index has long fed commercial search engines, which spider through these resources as they scour for web content. Another collaborative directory is ibiblio, which draws upon more than 1,000 volunteer contributors, who tend to specialize in a particular field. As ibiblio director Paul Jones explained, "We think specialists in their fields understand what they're doing better than librarians do. We collect the best people—and their work" (Jones, 2003). Another example is the Merlot Project, which relies upon a community of volunteer professors to judge and advance web content. Each contributing scholar manages a subject area and both annotates and rates selected websites. Perhaps the fastest-growing open source movement is wiki (*quick* in Hawaiian), a social software trend that enables any user to edit and build a given webpage within a wiki site. Wikipedia, for example, is a collaboratively built encyclopedia. Volunteer contributors change entries in an atmosphere of trust and public goodwill, and all former entries are archived so a user can see how a certain topic area has evolved.

Government-created subject gateways

A final and extremely important area of subject gateway activity involves government-driven projects. To date, the U.S. government has acted slowly and gingerly in coordinating web content for education. This is in part a result of minimal funding, but also in part because of a desire to do it right. Today, the most exciting federally

sponsored subject gateway projects in the United States are coming
from (or are being enabled by) the National Science Foundation. The
NSF is an apt place, perhaps, since it was this organization that
bankrolled the internet's backbone until 1995. Specifically, it's the
National Science Digital Library (NSDL), a branch of NSF, which has
been granting web content initiatives since 2000. Mostly interested in
funding projects related to undergraduate science education, the
NSDL awarded $13 million to about 80 proposals in 2000, and by 2003
was awarding $23–24 million to about 200 project proposals—mostly
projects aimed at making the digital science libraries of hundreds of
U.S. universities and colleges accessible via the NSDL.

Beyond funding these individual projects, the NSDL has part-
nered with a myriad of noncommercial and commercial databases and
services. Most are science related, including the Massachusetts
Institute of Technology's Dspace, a digital capturing, preservation,
and distribution network; PBS Science; INFOMINE; the *New York
Times'* Learning Network; and the Scientific Learning Corporation. In
addition to amassing a considerable subject gateway network to serve
undergraduate science, the NSDL is branching out (slowly) to the
humanities and K–12 audiences. Its partnership, for instance, with the
Internet Scout Project is an example of NSDL's potential as a national
gateway. Based at the University of Wisconsin, the Scout Project has
been compiling academic higher education and K–12 websites since
1994. According to NSDL director Lee Zia, a key goal is to begin providing organizational glue to pull together these archives and bridge
more relationships with the humanities, especially in connection with
the National Institute of Museum and Library Services. "The words
national and *science* are constraining us," he said, noting that despite
the potential for the NSDL to create a more inclusive portal, it does not
have a formal charter to move on to the nonscience areas. Regardless
of the NSDL's progress as a cohesive subject gateway, Zia has also
been content to go slowly and cautiously. Seeing the NSDL as an
organic, evolving creature, he fears that a well-meaning legislature
will likely act on the overpromise of the NSDL interface:

> I make an analogy with Wal-Mart in order to illustrate how we want
> to be careful about our expectations. When Wal-Mart opens up a
> store, they open up a whole store, not just lightbulbs in aisle 6. The
> NSDL is very different from a store that has a physicality to it . . .
> there are places to get stuff, there's a cash register. But in this new
> space, it will always evolve with the Net. Once people go there to

find something they can use, we have to make sure we have something to offer (Zia, personal communication, June 26, 2003).

Two possible futures await the NSDL, as current funding under the NSF remains tenuous. First, it could become like the Library of Congress: completely funded in perpetuity in the public good. Second, it could become quasi-independent like the Smithsonian, which has a nonprofit component and is supported through other institutions. Whether the NSDL remains resolutely in science or expands to a general education portal is another question. Currently, no other governmental body has moved to formally aggregate internet sites beyond the sciences.

While one would assume that the Library of Congress would be a natural place for coordinating and promoting a national subject gateway effort, the library has instead concentrated its efforts on making its primary source materials available online. Its digital preservation initiative includes the American Memory Collection, the Global Gateway, and America's Library, all of which feature rich collections of photographs, sound recordings, film clips, and other data that would otherwise remain deep within the library's archives. "We have the goods," said the library's digital reference specialist Elizabeth L. Brown, "and the library's mission is to now make these goods easily available via the internet" (Brown, personal communication, June 27, 2003). These digitization projects are significant contributions to education, but they focus inward rather than outward. And despite the value of this material, outreach efforts have been minimal: a summer education workshop for 50 teachers or librarians a year (since 1998) and a mailing to the social studies and English administrations in schools within the two counties around Washington, D.C.

The U.S. Department of Education has also begun some key subject gateway initiatives, but the focus is on teaching resources rather than organized links for students; the Gateway to Educational Materials (GEM), for example, provides access to more than 25,000 internet lesson plans, making it a one-stop browsing archive for teachers; the Federal Resources for Educational Excellence (FREE) is another teacher database that draws upon such governmental websites as the Library of Congress and the National Endowment for the Humanities; and the Virtual Reference Desk (VRD) is attempting to combine a web resource center—now painfully limited—with an option to email questions to librarians. In 2002 the U.S. Department of Education also began a 5-year project with the University of Syracuse, the University of Washington, and the Online Computer Library Center (OCLC) Institute to combine GEM and VRD and create a wide assortment of online education resources. Once again, the main goal is to reach and serve teachers. All these sites are still in their developmental phases and have a way to go before they are user-friendly.

Gateways in Europe and Australia

To date, nonprofit and government subject gateway projects throughout the United States have moved very slowly. Many nonprofit gateways, such as INFOMINE and the Internet Public Library, have directly competed against one another for the same limited grant money, a situation that has dampened the desire for collaboration. As Steve Mitchell, cocoordinator and managing editor of INFOMINE, remarked, "The U.S. has a lack of focus, a lack of organization. The economic challenges are starting to mount, and there's a lack of leadership and vision" (personal communication, June 12, 2003).

Although the government-supported subject gateway initiatives in the United States may be disconnected and not well funded, the European and Australian counterparts have benefited from a strong vision, collaboration, and healthy funding, especially in the area of higher education. The Dutch Electronic Subject Service (DutchESS); the Finnish Virtual Library (FVL), the Education Network Australia (EDNA), and the United Kingdom's Resource Discovery Network, for example, are all nationally supported subject gateway systems. Collaboration has come easy because both the education systems and the funding arrangements are centralized. Instead of being funded by grants, every involved institution operates under contracts.

Britain's Resource Discovery Network (RDN), for example, is supported through especially generous funding from the Higher Education Funding Councils for England, Scotland, and Wales. Universities throughout the United Kingdom are responsible for the growth and update of particular subject areas: ALTIS (University of Birmingham) deals with hospitality, leisure, sport, and tourism; BIOME (University of Nottingham) covers health and life sciences; EEVL (Heriot Watt University in Edinburgh) handles engineering, mathematics, and computing; GEsource (the Consortium of Academic

Libraries in Manchester) is concerned with geography and environment; Humbul (Oxford University) is taking on humanities; PSIgate (also located with the Consortium of Academic Libraries in Manchester) manages physical sciences, and SOSIG (University of Bristol) is responsible for social sciences, business, and law. Each of these university hubs is amassing thousands of "authoritative" academic web resources on their assigned subject areas, with hundreds of active content experts from more than 70 educational and research organizations contributing web links. The RDN initiative is actually only a small part of the United Kingdom's larger Electronic Libraries (eLib) Programme, which is lavishing significant funds on academic libraries and institutions to digitize special collections, including theses and all forms of academic research. "The main remit is to provide a body of tangible, electronic resources and services for U.K. Higher Education," an introduction to the eLib programme reads, "and to affect a cultural shift toward the acceptance and use of said resources and services in place of more traditional information storage and access methods" ("Introduction," 2001). The United States has not reached this level of coordination, because its universities and colleges are either state or private entities (hence more discrete), and because the various independent subject gateway initiatives are grant, not contract, based, allowing for more creativity and innovation, perhaps, but also less consolidation and communication.

Even with widespread efforts to organize the web for noncommercial and research purposes, all subject gateways—even the ones in the United Kingdom, will only be successful if people know about them and use them. At least in the United States, subject gateway initiatives—especially the one dependent on state, rather than federal, support—continuously struggle for funding. And without funding, commercial alternatives will surely have the upper hand. For example, a number of professors participating in the Merlot Project worry that corporate partnerships and advertising loom on the horizon, threatening the project's independence and usefulness. The difficulty, of course, is to generate public awareness about the existence of noncommercial directories and why they are important to the future of the web and democracy. Merlot Project contributors do what they can to spread the word; one of their tactics is to wear buttons at conferences that say, "Ask Me About Merlot." "I joke that it's like Amway," Merlot director Gerard L. Hanley told the *Chronicle for Higher Education*. "You get one person who then goes and sells to five other people, who each go and sell to five other people. As the math guys know, that's exponential—that's good" (Young, 2002).

In their book *Watch It: The Risks and Promises of Information Technologies* (2000), Nicholas Burbules and Thomas Callister advise against subject gateways, seeing these tools as a way of censoring content—limiting the kinds of material available on the web. Accordingly, they see any government-sponsored initiatives to set aside corners of the internet as nonprofit sectors, or, in their words, "charitable zones" along the lines of PBS, to be misguided, and even dangerous. "Certainly," they write, "government intervention raises its own dangers of ideological control" (p. 145).

But in the same breath, Burbules and Callister speak alarmingly at the future of online content that continues to be dominated by commercial interests:

> Who will sponsor the unpopular, the challenging, the critical voices that disagree with the interests and outlook of the sponsors? Who, for example, will sponsor the anti-McDonald's site? To what extent is the internet playing a role in instilling users with a more commercial mindset themselves, becoming more enmeshed in the operations of capitalism? . . . Are schools in the business of inculcating students with the spirit of unbridled capitalism? Who gave them this charge? (p. 146)

The authors are well aware of the internet's evolution toward a medium that reflects the current state of television and radio. But by disregarding the efforts of so many nonprofit subject gateways to make valuable content available and accessible, they are letting commercial interests have the last word. Although they sometimes fall short of their alternative mission (Schechter, 1999), where else but on PBS and National Public Radio (NPR) is there television and radio content that goes beyond boundaries and addresses unpopular ideas? Both networks, however, have to sweat every time they actually raise an unpopular idea. As Balas (1999) relates, the fight to retroactively create a public broadcasting service in 1967 after television and radio were entrenched in commercial interests was not an easy one, and the results—a compromised PBS network serving "high-culture" tastes and offering programming marked by corporate sponsorship—fit a narrow definition of democratic expression. In fact, the major failing of PBS and NPR is that they are "public" in name only. In practice, the vast majority of their funding is private and predominantly from corporations, which affect their range of programming perspective.

Perhaps an even better example of a public forum are the nation's public libraries. Where else but in public libraries, including those in public schools and universities, can we find books that lead us to truly in-depth, unconventional, and controversial subject matter? Even as the future internet looks more and more like commercial television, the metaphor that has sustained the medium's development has been the library—not a commercial bookstore, where only the popular is stocked—but a government-supported public library, where ideas are shared with less regard to their marketability.

Despite Burbules and Callister's concerns of censorship—indeed, public broadcasting is prone to political meddling (Schechter, 1999) and public libraries are subject to persistent censorship challenges (ALA, 2002)—publicly supported media institutions still are able to present ideas that step outside the bounds of commercial media. On one level, a public internet directory/portal would attempt to bring together the efforts of the many individuals and organizations that are busily working on maintaining links to websites that may otherwise be sent to the margins. An effective directory/portal would also help students juxtapose the misinformation, malinformation, commercially sponsored information, and irrelevant websites—the real-world stuff popular among proponents of critical-reading skills—so students can better make sense of our world. The potential of a noncommercial educational portal to help students understand the world we live in is enormous, in that it could provide a critical distance from the commercial spin of our everyday surroundings.

Interestingly, a publicly funded national portal geared towards research and education has been proposed. Lawrence Grossman, former head of NBC News and PBS, and Newton Minow, former FCC Chair who famously called television a "vast wasteland," began promoting the idea of a Digital Opportunity Investment Trust, or DO IT, in 2000. As they have aptly argued in *A Digital Gift to the Nation*, "market forces alone cannot fulfill all the essential needs of our citizens for formal and informal education, lifelong learning, civic and political information, health information, and arts and culture" (Grossman & Minow, 2001, p. 12). The national project would entail setting up a trust fund based on money generated by spectrum auctions as broadcasters convert from analog to digital signals. The trust would be set up in a similar manner as the National Science Foundation, and would issue grants towards the development a nonprofit digital content portal "to help ensure that much of what is most important on the Internet is kept open and readily accessible to all" (p. 17). The DO IT initiative has historical precedents: the Northwest Ordinance (1787), which used proceeds from public land sales to establish public schools; the Morrill Act (1872), which used similar land sale funds to establish 105 land-grant colleges across the United States, and the G.I. Bill (1944), which enabled millions of World War II veterans to attend college. Grossman and Minow believe that the sales of the public airwaves should be used, in part, to finance long-lasting public projects that would enhance U.S. democracy. "Why not make that money last a lifetime, several millions of them, by reinvesting it in an educational 'land-grant of the airwaves,' thus making it an invaluable asset for the nation's future?" they ask (p. 16).

Since 2002, various senators and representatives have endorsed the idea. In 2002, Senators Christopher Dodd (Democrat, from Connecticut) and Jim Jeffords (Independent, from Vermont) introduced S. 2603, and Representative Ed Markey (Democrat, from Massachusetts) introduced H.R. 4641. Both bills would have devoted 50% of all future spectrum auction proceeds towards the digital trust fund, but neither got out of committee. The idea was introduced again in 2003 as S. 1854 by sponsors Senator Dodd, Senator Olympia Snowe (Republican, from Maine), and Senator Richard Durbin (Democrat, from Illionois). This time the bill asked for a 30% portion of the auctions to benefit the trust. As appealing as these bills are, they face a tremendous uphill battle unless the larger public—especially educators—stand behind them and argue for their relevance. Otherwise, Congress will likely use the billions in revenues from spectrum auctions for balancing the budget, paying for tax cuts, and fighting "the war on terrorism." Unfortunately, not one mainstream newspaper, wire report, or news network even carried a mention of the bill as it was introduced on Capitol Hill in November 2003.

THE QUIET REVOLUTION

For the short term, educators should begin to direct their students to use the considerable library-based, citizen-based, and government-supported subject gateway efforts that are now taking form. The one glaring problem, however, is that students don't like to use subject gateways. They don't like to deep-link, finding this process disorienting and unwieldy, no matter how useful the material they might eventually locate. Moreover, users are so conditioned to hop on search engine portals and access the "whole web" that it would take a lot to affect a cultural shift toward subject gateway use; the appeal of immediate search engine results would win over every time. The good news is that solutions to these problems are coming fast and furious from the digital library and computer science communities. In fact, a new set of technology protocols and services are promising to reinvigorate subject gateways, creating a movement that just might bode well for education and the information superhighway.

The buzz among a growing community of librarians is cross-searching: the ability to search across many subject gateway platforms at the same time. This new searching method looks and feels a lot like a search engine. Users type in keywords and dynamically search (librarians like the word *harvest*) across hundreds, even thousands, of different subject gateways located all over the web. If search engines crawl over an index, cross-searching tools harvest a database collective—a collective that could serve commercial or educational purposes. This technology is revolutionary because it has huge implications for the comprehensiveness and relevance of search results. In fact, a user (let's say a student) could enter a search-engine–like environment, access thousands of academic sites, and not come across a single commercial entity.

The seeds of this movement have been around for some time. Since 1988, engineers have been experimenting with ways to link metadata (databases with rich text files) within a library's own interface using protocols such as the Lightweight Directory Access Protocol (LDAP), the Common Indexing Protocol (CIP), and z39.50. But more recently, a new cross-searching framework, called (in a rather cumbersome manner) the Open Archive Initiative Protocol for Metadata Harvesting (OAI-PMH), is one interoperability system being heavily tested in projects around the United States and throughout Europe. Beginning in 1999 as a way to spur discussions about maintaining, indexing, and searching distributed collections of metadata, the OAI-PMH (OAI for short) system depends upon subject gateways to be "OAI compliant." Once they achieve this compliance, they can be searched by way of a single database.

Meanwhile, other systems are emerging that can work alongside (or separate from) OAI for other cross-platform search options. One of these is iVia, an open source virtual library system developed by the people at INFOMINE. This is a very promising hybrid system that combines resources from expert-based subject gateways with resources from a search engine crawler. IVia identifies and provides descriptive information for important sites, a process that, in turn, helps users find these sites. It does much of this automatically. As its creators write, "Systems like iVia may prove critical within the larger context of enabling those in the learning community, among others, to continue to reliably find what they need on the Internet" (Mitchell et al., 2003).

In the United States, the NSF and the privately funded Mellon Foundation are behind the OAI initiative, seeing it work in conjunction with other harvesting, search engine, and cataloging efforts. Mellon has allocated $1.5 million toward seven major OAI trials. One of them, developed by the University of Michigan Digital Library Production Services, is OAIster (pronounced "oyster," www.oaister.org), a vast collection of digital resources (including Taiwanese text archives, numerous map and photo collections, German theses, even a collection of sound recordings of Native Alaskan speakers). By 2003 more than 185 obscure databases had become "OAI enabled" to join the OAIster collective (their slogan: "Find the pearls"). The NSF is also pushing to integrate OAI into the numerous subject gateways it has collected under the National Science Digital Library. Moreover, various organizations, such as the Coalition for Networked Information (CNI) and the Joint Conference on Digital Libraries (JCDL), are providing important international and national forums to discuss the "transformative promise of networked information technology" ("Coalition," 2003). Once again, gateway efforts across Europe are more organized and fully funded than in the United States. The United Kingdom has united all its RDN hubs in an OAI-compliant collective, which in turn has been absorbed by the Renardus portal, a service funded by the European Union to unite high-quality internet resources for higher education throughout all of Europe.

A variety of portal software programs, such as the Scout Portal Toolkit in the United States and the PORTAL Project in the United Kingdom, are also encouraging subject gateway portal development that will help organizations build subject gateways with minimal effort and add to the burgeoning subject gateway community. Commercial companies are also getting in on the act. The company Ex Libris, for example, offers a cross-searching portal called MetaLib;

Fretwell Downing has developed the Z-portal interface. This is just a sampling of the many developments—protocol, portal, and network—that have arisen to advance subject gateway initiatives over the past few years.

Not surprisingly, there have been, and continue to be, difficulties with cross-searching technology. One of these is deciding on a common protocol. OAI might quickly fade if it can't adequately handle resource duplication between gateways. Then there is a question of standardizing subject headings and figuring out ways to customize a subject gateway collective to different user groups. As Sue Davidsen of the Internet Public Library pointed out, the gateways geared toward higher education speak a different language from those geared toward the K–12 community. A user's ability to choose different intellectual levels and languages is something, according to some librarians, that needs to be worked out (Davidsen, personal communication, June 13, 2003).

But perhaps the mixing of levels is a good thing: It might allow students to feel that they're dabbling in the "real world" of academic information, legitimizing the cross-searching portal as an all-encompassing academic navigation tool. Then again, it might turn them off subject gateways completely. In any case, librarians, engineers, and computer scientists are in the early stages of this quiet revolution.

The OAI is just one promising development to make U. S. subject gateways less scattered. But until there is a national policy for organizing educational internet content that even approaches the scale of the "educational challenge" to wire every school, vast amounts of online information—conflicting opinions, multiple voices, and rich primary resources (the seeds for critical inquiry)—will be undetected and underused. Organizing web content is the next educational challenge. Let the work begin.

Comprehension and Perception/ Information Literacy

CHECKLIST FOR EVALUATING ONLINE INFORMATION

As you navigate the internet and retrieve information for your class assignments and research papers, it's important to question the truthfulness of this information.[1] Is it trustworthy? Who wrote it? Why did they write it?

This checklist will help you in your quest to be sure that all the information you obtain from the online world is "good" and useful in your studies.

What is the source of the information?

Many times, a site's address will provide some clues. A legitimate information provider will have a straightforward online address, such as http://www.microsoft.com. On the other hand, an individual user will have an online address reading something like http://www.xyz.com/~smith/position.html. The ~smith part of the address gives it away. In this case, an individual named Smith has put webpages in his or her personal directory and made their contents available to the world.

Why is this information online?

Authors put information online for a reason. Ask yourself if the purpose is to inform and educate internet users about a particular topic, or if there is some kind of hidden agenda.

---

[1] Adapted from *Classroom Connect* (1996, September). Student handout: Information literacy: Checklist for evaluating online information. [Online], http://www.classroom.net.

Who wrote the information, and what is the point of view of the writer?

These are the two most telling questions. If you've never heard of the author or if the information wasn't well written, chances are you should do more research into his or her background before accepting the information as factual. Go to an internet search engine (such as http://www.altavista.digital.com) and type in the author's name. What comes up? What else have they published? Check the library to see if this person has published anything in the real world.

Does the online information contain links to other sites, and do they reveal any biases of the author?

Following the links online that authors place inside their online information is one of the best ways to discover more about the author. These links may also reveal any biases of an author.

How recent is the information?

While new information is not necessarily any more accurate than old information, this is still an important question to answer. If you're doing a report on the current state of the former Soviet Union, steer clear of any information that was put on the internet before 1991.

Other questions to ask:

- Who is the main audience for this information?
- How often is the site/information updated?
- How does this site compare with others that deal with the same subject matter?
- Does the text follow basic rules of grammar, spelling, and literary composition?
- How knowledgeable is the individual or group on the subject matter of the site?
- Is contact information for the author or producer included in the document so you can email the person with questions or comments?
- What is the value of the website in comparison to the range of Library Media Center resources available on the topic you're researching?
- Does the author of the online information cite his or her sources in the document so you can check them for authenticity?

Noncommercial Subject Gateway Efforts Mentioned in the Text

Librarian-supported Subject Gateways

Internet Public Library
INFOMINE
Internet Scout Report
KidsClick
Librarian's Index to the Internet
Michigan eLibrary

Citizen-supported Subject Gateways

ibiblio
Merlot Project
Open Directory Project
Wikipedia

Government-supported Subject Gateways

National Science Digital Library (NSDL)
Library of Congress
  • The American Memory Collection
  • The Global Gateway
  • America's Library
The Gateway to Educational Materials (GEM)
Federal Resources for Educational Excellence (FREE)

Subject Gateways in Europe and Australia

Dutch Electronic Subject Service (DutchESS)
Education Network Australia (EDNA)
Finnish Virtual Library (FVL)

Resource Discovery Network (RDN)
- ALTIS
- BIOME
- EEVL
- GESource
- Humbul
- PSIGate
- SOSIG

Portal-building Initiatives

Scout Portal Toolkit
PORTAL Project (U.K.)
Ex Libris
MetaLib
Z-portal

Cross-sharing Initiatives

Dublin Core Metadata Initiative
Lightweight Directory Access Protocol (LDAP)
Common Indexing Protocol (CIP)
Open Archive Initiative Protocol for Metadata Harvesting (OAI-PMH)
OAIster
Ivia

Other Resources

Coalition for Networked Information (CNI)
Joint Conference on Digital Libraries (JCDL)
Ariadne online magazine
D-Lib Magazine
Digital Promise

References

About Link Brokerage.com. (2003). LinkBrokerage.com [Online]. Available: http://www.linkbrokerage.com [2003, May 27].

About the Open Directory Project. *The Open Directory Project* [Online]. Available: http://dmoz.org/about.html [2003, June 21].

ALA. (2002). Banned books week. *American Library Association* [Online]. Available: http://www.ala.org/bbooks/challeng.html [2002, January 12].

Alexander, D., & Dichter, A. (2000, April 18). Ads and kids: How young is too young? *Mediachannel.org* [Online]. Available: http://www.mediachannel.org/ atissue/consumingkids/frong.shtml [2001, June 29].

Alexander, J. E., & Tate, M. A. (1999). *Web wisdom: How to evaluate and create information quality on the web*. Mahwah, NJ: Lawrence Erlbaum Associates.

AOL. (2001, November 14). Governor Ray Barnes, America Online and Turner Broadcasting announce initiative to use AOL@SCHOOL statewide. Press release. *AOL Time Warner* [Online]. Available: http://media.aoltimewarner.com/media/ cb_press_view.cfm?release_num=55252296 [2002, February 11].

AOL. (2002, June 19). AOL@School reaches more than 36% of K–12 schools in two years (2002, June 19). Press release. AOL Time Warner [Online]. Available: http://media.aoltimewarner.com/media/press_view.cfm?release_num=55252629 [2003, June 21].

Arnold, J. M., & Jayne, E. A. (1998, January). Dangling by a slender thread: The lessons and implications of teaching the worldwide web to Freshmen. *The Journal of Academic Librarianship, 24*(1), 43–52.

Associated Press. (2000, May 16). Survey: Kids OK with giving personal facts out on the web. *The Waterloo/Cedar Falls Courier*, p. A2.

Associated Press. (2002, July 12). Search engines not recognizing advertisers' preferred treatment. *Waterloo/Cedar Falls Courier*, p. D4.

Atkinson, C. (1938). *Education by radio in American schools*. Nashville, TN: George Peabody College for Teachers.

Aufderheide, P. (1999). *Communications policy and the public interest: The telecommunications act of 1996*. New York: Guilford Press.

Bailey, G. D., & Lumley, D. (1999, January). Fishing the Net. *Electronic School*, A20–A23. [Online]. Available: www.electronic-school.com.

Baird, Z. (2002, November/December). Governing the Internet. *Foreign Affairs, 81*(6), pp. 15–20. [Online]. Available: http://www.markle.org.

Balas, G. R. (1999). *The recovery of institutional vision for U.S. public media: Three moments of purpose and failed resolve*. Unpublished doctoral dissertation, University of Iowa.

Berger, P. (1998). *Internet for active learners: Curriculum-based strategies for K–12*. Chicago: American Library Association.

Berners-Lee, T. (2002). Japan Prize Commemorative Lecture [Online]. Available: http://www.w3.org/2002/04/Japan/Lecture.html [February 6, 2004].

Beuick, M. D. (1927). The limited social effect of radio broadcasting. *American Journal of Sociology, 32*, 615–622.

Bos, N. (2000). High school students' critical evaluation of scientific resources on the world wide web. *Journal of Science Education and Technology, 9*(2),161–173.

Brandt, D. S. (1996a, May). Evaluating information on the Internet. *Computers in Libraries, 16*(4), 44–46.

Brandt, D. S. (1996b, September). Relevancy and searching the Internet. *Computers in Libraries, 16*(8), 35–39.

Bruno, R. B., & Gerrity, M. (2000, September). The big picture. *Yahoo! Internet Life, 6*(9), 93–95.

Building a stronger, hi-tech, deregulated economy. (1993, August 16). *White House Publications* [Online]. Available: http://clinton1.nara.gov/White_House/Publications/html/briefs/ii-6-plain.html [August 12, 2003].

Burbules, N. C., & Callister, T. A., Jr. (2000). *Watch it: The risks and promises of information technologies for education*. Boulder, CO: Westview Press.

Burstein, D., & Kline, D. (1995). *Road warriors: Dreams and nightmares along the information highway*. New York: Dutton.

Campbell, R., Martin, C., & Fabos, B. (2003). *Media and culture: An introduction to mass communications*. New York: Bedford/St. Martin's Press.

Carey, J. (1997). *James Carey: A critical reader*. Minneapolis: University of Minnesota Press.

Cervetti, G., Pardales, M. J., & Damico, J. S. (2001, April). A tale of differences: Comparing traditions, perspectives, and educational goals of critical reading and critical literacy. *Reading Online, 4*(9) [Online]. Available: http://www.readingonline.org/articles/art_index.asp?HREF=/articles/cervetti/index.html [2002, February].

Clausing, J. (1999, July 20). Study says most children's web sites are lax on privacy. *New York Times on the Web* [Online]. Available: http://www.nytimes.com/library/tech/99/07/cyber/articles/20privacy-day.html [1999, July 20].

Claus-Smith, D. (1999, November/December). Starting small, dreaming big : The OSLIS Project brings resources statewide. *Multimedia Schools, 6*(5), 29–31.

Clinton, President B. (1997a). Clinton announces electronic commerce initiative [Online]. Available: http://Clinton3.nara.gov/WH/New/Commerce/message.html [2002, April 5].

Clinton, President B. (1997b). State of the Union Address, February 4.

Coalition asks states to protect children from ZapMe! Corp. Privacy invasion (2000, January 19). In *Commercial Alert* [Online]. Available: http://www.commercialalert.org/releases/zapmepackrel.html [2001, March 25].

Collins, F. A. (1912). *The wireless man*. New York: Century.

CommerceNet. (1997, December 11). Electronic commerce on the rise according to CommerceNet/Nielsen Media research survey. Press release. *CommerceNet* [Online]. Available: http://www.commerce.net/news/press/121197.html [2001, April 30].

Connecting every pupil to the world. (1995, December 28). *New York Times*, Sec. A, p. 20.

Cuban, L. (1986). *Teachers and machines: The classroom use of technology since 1920*. New York: Teachers College Press.

Darrow, B. H. (1932). *Radio: The assistant teacher.* Columbus, OH: R. G. Adams.

Douglas, S. (1987). *Inventing American broadcasting, 1899–1922.* Baltimore, MD: Johns Hopkins University Press.

Ebersole, S. (2000, September). Uses and gratifications of the web among students. *Journal of Computer-Mediated Communication, 6*(1) [Online]. Available: http://www.ascusc.org/jcmc/vol6/issue1/ebersole.html [2003, May 18].

Education by Radio. (1931, March 26). *1,* 25.

EGS link exchange. (2003). *EGS Brokerage* [Online]. Available: http://www.egsbroker-age.com/health-insurance-linkinfo.htm [2003, May 27].

Ehrenreich, B. (1989). *Fear of falling: The inner life of the middle class.* New York: HarperPerennial.

Elkin, T. (2003, April 14). Marketers key in to search; Companies find the tool efficient to reach customers. *Advertising Age,* p. 42.

Fabos, B. (2000, May). ZapMe! zaps you. *Journal of Adolescent & Adult Literacy, 43*(8), 720–725.

Fones-Wolf, E. A. (1994). *Selling free enterprise: The business assault on labor and liberalism, 1945–60.* Urbana, IL: University of Illinois Press.

Fox, R. F. (1996). *Harvesting minds: How TV commercials control kids.* Westport, CT: Praeger.

Francisco, B. (2003, June 19). Microsoft launches its own web crawler. *CBS MarketWatch* [Online]. Available: http://aol.marketwatch.com/news/ [2003, June 21].

Frechette, J. (2002). *Developing media literacy in cyberspace: Pedagogy and critical learning for the twenty-first-century classroom.* Westport, CT: Praeger.

Frost, S. E. (1937). *Education's own stations: The history of broadcast licenses issued to educational institutions.* Chicago: University of Chicago Press.

Gaither, C. (2003, February 23). Searching for dollars as banner market flags, Net giants pin hopes on revenue from targeted ads related to specific queries. *The Boston Globe,* p. F1.

Gardner, S. A., Benham, H. H., & Newell, B. M. (1999, September). Oh, what a tangled web we've woven! Helping students evaluate web sources. *English Journal, 89*(1), 39–44.

Gates, B. (1995). *The road ahead.* New York: Viking.

Gee, J. P. (2000, February). Teenagers in new times: A new literacy studies perspective. *Journal of Adolescent and Adult Literacy, 43*(5), 412–420.

Gibson, S., & Tranter, J. (2000, Summer). Internet information: The whole truth? *Canadian Social Studies, 34*(4), pp. 77–80.

Gordon, D. (1942). *All children listen.* New York: George W. Stewart.

Grassian, E. (2000). Thinking critically about world wide web resources. *UCLA College Library* [Online]. Available: http://www.library.ucla.edu/libraries/college/help/critical/index.htm [2000, November 6].

Griffiths, J. R., & Brophy, P. (2002, October 10). Student searching behavior in the JISC Information Environment. *Ariadne, 33* [Online]. Available: http://www.ariadne.ac.uk/issue33/edner/intro.html [2003, June 3].

Grossman, L. K., & Minow, N. N. (2001). *A digital gift to the nation: Fulfilling the promise of the digital and internet age.* New York: Century Foundation Press.

Harmsen, S. (2003, Spring). The Internet and your health: Case study on ephedra. Critical process project, University of Northern Iowa.

Harris, R. (1997, November). Evaluating Internet research sources. *Vanguard University of South California* [Online]. Available: http://www.vanguard.edu/rharris/evalu8it.htm [2000, November 6].

Harvey, F. (2003a, January 15). Online ads await click-through to profitability: Questions have been raised about whether the medium works, but analysts are optimistic. *Financial Times*, FT Report, p. 1.

Harvey, F. (2003b, March 4). Putting a price on results: Recent acquisitions suggest the sponsored search sector is a bright spot in a gloomy market. *The Financial Times*, p. 32.

Hays, C. L. (1999, December 5). Channel One's mixed grades in schools. *The New York Times*, Sec. 3, pp. 1, 14–15.

Henderson, J. R. (2000, June 13). ICYouSee: T is for thinking. *Ithaca College Library* [Online]. Available: http://www.ithaca.edu/library/Training/hott.html [2000, November 7]

Hill, F. E. (1942). *Tune in for education*. New York: National Committee on Education by Radio.

Hinman, H., & Leita, C. (1999). Librarians' index to the internet (LII). In A. Wells, S. Calcari, & T. Koplow (Eds.), *The amazing Internet challenge: How leading projects use library skills to organize the web* (pp. 144–160). Chicago: American Library Association.

Hoffman, D. (1995). The challenges of electronic commerce. *Hotwired* [Online]. Available: http://hotwired.lycos.com/i-agent/95/21/index3a.html [2000, March 5].

Holmes, J. (2002, July 9). Syracuse University awarded $5 million contract from the U.S. Department of Education for digital library services. Press release. *Information Institute of Syracuse* [Online]. Available: http://iis.syr.edu/ press_releases/contract.shtml [2003, June 18].

Holt, G. (1995, September 15). Catalog outsourcing: No clear cut choice. *Library Journal*, 120(15), 32–34.

Hunter, P. (2002, October). Exploring the information environment, Editorial. *Ariadne*, 33 [Online]. Available: http://www.ariadne.ac.uk/issue33/editorial/intro.html [2003, June 10].

Ickes, H. (1936). In C. S. Marsh (Ed.), *Educational broadcasting 1936: Proceedings of the first national conference on educational broadcasting* (pp. 7–14). Chicago: University of Chicago Press.

Imind—the parody. (2003) [Online]. Available: http://www.fabiangonzalez.com /imind/ [2003, June 2].

Information literacy and the Internet: How to sort "good" online information from the bad. (1996, September). *Classroom Connect (The K–12 educator's practical guide to using the Internet and commercial online services)*, 1, 4–5.

Internet activities. (2002, December). *Pew Internet and American Life Project* [Online]. Available: http://www.pewInternet.org/reports/chart.asp?img= Internet_A8.htm [2003, May 28].

Introduction to eLib: The Electonic Libraries Programme (2001, October 18). *UKOLN* [Online]. Available: http://www.ukoln.ac.uk/services/elib/ [2003, June 18].

Jowett, G. S., Jarvie, I. C., & Fuller, K. H. (1996). *Children and the movies: Media influence and the Payne Fund controversy*. Cambridge, England: Cambridge University Press.

Jupiter Communications. (2000, Sept. 13). Jupiter: Internet to influence U.S. kids and teens off-line spending, $21.4 billion expected in 2005. Press release. *Jupiter Communications* [Online]. Available: www.jmm.com/xp/jmm/press/2000/ pr_091300.xml [2002, March 22].

Kapitzke, C. (2001, February). Information literacy: The changing library. *Journal of Adolescent & Adult Literacy*, 44(5), 450–456.

Kapoun, J. (1998, July/August). Teaching undergrads web evaluation. *College and Research Libraries, 59*(7), 522–523.

Kellner, D. (1990). *Television and the crises of democracy.* Boulder, CO: Westview Press.

Kennedy, S. D. (1998). *Best bet Internet: Reference and research when you don't have time to mess around.* Chicago: American Library Association.

Kirk, E. E. (2000, January 4). Evaluating information found on the Internet. *University of St. Thomas (St. Paul, MN) Milton S. Eisenhower Library* [Online]. Available: http://milton.mse.jhu.edu:8001/research/education/net.html [2000, November 6].

Kirkwood, H. P. (1998, July/August). Beyond evaluation: A model for cooperative evaluation of Internet resources. *Online, 22*(4), 66–84.

Kohut, R. (2000, March). MetaSearching the Net. *Learning and Leading with Technology, 27*(6), 18–21.

Konrad, R. (2002, July 3). Teen market clicks past e-tailers. *CNET News* [Online]. Available: http://news.com.com/2100-1017-941731.html [2003, May 29].

Kurtz, H. (2000, November 4). Bulk of state's teachers use computers, More than 97% of schools have Internet access. *Denver Rocky Mountain News,* p. 27A.

Lambeth, J. (2001, August 2). A plague on your pop-ups: Adverts on the web can be a trial but the online world is seeking new ways to torment. *The Daily Telegraph,* p. 2.

Lankshear, C., Snyder, I., & Green, B. (2000). *Teachers and technoliteracy: Managing literacy, technology, and learning in schools.* St. Leonards, NSW: Allen & Unwin.

Lasica, J. D. (2001, July 23). Search engines and editorial integrity. *Online Journalism Review* [Online]. Available: http://www.ojr.org/ojr/technology/1017778969.php [2001, December 12].

Lawrence, S., & Giles, C. L. (1999, July 8). Accessibility of information on the web. *Nature, 400*(6740), 107–109.

Levenson, W. B., & Stasheff, E. (1952). *Teaching through radio and television.* (Rev. ed.) New York: Rinehart.

Levin, D., & Arafeh, S. (2002, August 14). The digital disconnect: The widening gap between Internet-savvy students and their schools. *The Pew Internet & American Life Project* [Washington, DC] [Online]. Available: http://www.pewinternet.org.

Luke, A. (2000, February). Critical literacy in Australia: A matter of context and standpoint. *Journal of Adolescent and Adult Literacy, 43*(5), 448–459.

Luke, C. (1990). *Constructing the child viewer: A history of the American discourse on television and children, 1950–1980.* New York: Praeger.

Luke, C. (2000, February). New literacies in teacher education. *Journal of Adolescent and Adult Literacy, 43*(5), 424–435.

MacKay, P. (2003, April 1). In search of . . . the perfect search. *Technology & Learning, 23*(9), 34–35.

Marsh, C. S. (Ed.). (1936). *Educational broadcasting 1936: Proceedings of the first national conference on educational broadcasting.* Chicago: University of Chicago Press.

Mather, P. (1996, December 11). Critical literacy: The WWW's great potential. *University of Vermont* [Online]. Available: http://ei.cs.vt.edu/%7Ewwwbtb/book/chap6/critical.html [2000, November 6].

Mayer, M. (1963, September 14). Last chance for our schools? *The Saturday Evening Post, 236*(31), 24–36.

McChesney, R. W. (1994). *Telecommunications, mass media, and democracy: The battle for the control of U.S. broadcasting, 1928–1935.* London: Oxford University Press.

McChesney, R. W. (1997). *Corporate media and the threat to democracy.* New York: Seven Stories Press.

McChesney, R. (1999). *Rich media, poor democracy: Communication politics in dubious times.* Chicago: University of Illinois Press.

McChesney, R., Wood, E. M., & Foster, J. B. (1998). *Capitalism and the information age: The political economy of the global communication revolution.* New York: Monthly Review Press.

McClusky, F. D. (1937). *Motion pictures for the schools.* Unpublished report presented to the Rockefeller Foundation, 1937.

McCurry, M. (1995, September 21). Press briefing by assistant to the secretary of commerce Jonathan Sallet. The Exploratorium, San Francisco, CA.

McKibben, B. (1992). *The age of missing information.* New York: Plume.

McNeal, J. U. (1992). *Kids as customers: A handbook of marketing to children.* New York: Lexington Books.

Microsoft. (1995, November 28). The connected learning community. Press release. *Microsoft Corporation* [Online]. Available: http://www.gsn.org/site /new/gsh-press.html [2002, April 5].

Minkel, W. (2000, October). Burden of spoof. *School Library Journal, 46*(10), p. 49.

Mitchell, S., & Mooney, M. (1999). INFOMINE. In A. Wells, S. Calcari, & T. Koplow (Eds.), *The amazing Internet challenge: How leading projects use library skills to organize the web* (pp. 97–120). Chicago: American Library Association.

Mitchell, S., Moony, M., Mason, J., Paynter, G. W., Ruscheinski, J., Kedzierski, A., & Humphreys, K. (2003, January). IVia open source virtual library system. *D-Lib Magazine, 9*(1), 1–13.

Moje, E. B., Young, J. P., Readence, J. E., & Moore, D. W. (2000, February). Reinventing adolescent literacy for new times: Perennial and millenial issues. *Journal of Adolescent and Adult Literacy, 43*(5), 400–410.

Molnar, A. (1996). *Giving kids the business: Commercialization of America's schools.* New York: Westview Press.

MoreVisibility platform three: E-commerce initiative. (2003). *MoreVisibility.com* [Online]. Available: http://www.morevisibility.com/services_three.html [2003, April 18].

Morton, R. A. (1910, January 15). The amateur wireless operator. *Outlook, 94,* 131.

NFO WorldGroup. (2001, August 15). Kids are strong influencers on where to go, what to buy. *NFO* [Online]. Available: http://www.nfow.com/pr081501.asp. [2002, March 25].

Noakes, A. (1999). Argus Clearinghouse (Argus). In A. Wells, S. Calcari, & T. Koplow (Eds.), *The amazing Internet challenge: How leading projects use library skills to organize the web* (pp. 17–35). Chicago: American Library Association.

Nunberg, G. (2003, May 18). As Google goes, so goes the nation. *The New York Times* [Online]. Available: http://www.nytimes.com/2003/05/18/weekinreview/18NUNB.html [2003, May 18]

Oder, N. (2000, October 1). Cataloguing the Net: Two years later. *Library Journal, 125*(16), 50–51.

O'Leary, M. (1998, July/August). Web directories demonstrate an enduring online law. *Online, 22*(4), 79–81.

Ormondroyd, J., Engle, M., & Cosgrave, T. (2000, June 21). How to critically analyze information sources. *Reference Services Division, Cornell University Library* [Online]. Available: http//www.library.cornell.edu/okuref/research/ skill26.htm [2000, November 6].

Overture. (2001). *Search Performance* [Online]. Available: http://www.overture.com /d/specials/welcome.jhtml;$sessionid$W5EQVSQAA2BH3QFIEOOAPUQ [2002, January 6].

Overture. (2003a, February 25). Overture to acquire web search unit of Fast Search & Transfer—FAST. Press release. *Overture, Inc.* [Online]. Available: http://www.corporate-ir.net/ireye/ir_site.zhtml?ticker=OVER&script= 410&layout=0&item_id=385605 [2003, April 18].

Overture. (2003b). Vision: Corporate overview. *Overture, Inc.* [Online]. Available: http://www.content.overture.com/d/Usm/about/company/vision.jhtml [2003, May 25].

Overture. (2003c, October 17). Overture and Microsoft extend search distribution relationship in the U.S. and U.K. *Press release. Overture, Inc.* [Online]. Available: http://www.corporate-ir.net/ireye/ir_site.zhtml?ticker=OVER& script=410&layout=-6&item_id=459799 [2003, November 17].

Parija, B. (1999, December 8). ZapMe! launches ZapMall. *WITCapital Company Report* [Online]. Available: http://www.witcapital.com/research/researchbody.jsp? Report=/izap_19991208 [2001, November 8].

Paul, N., & Williams, M. (1999). *Great Scouts! CyberGuides for subject searching on the web.* Medford, NJ: CyberAge Books.

Penkava, M. (1999, November 15). Internet profiling and privacy. *Talk of the Nation.* Transcript.

Pollan, M. (2001). *The botany of desire: A plant's eye view of the world.* New York: Random House.

Pugh, T. (2000, June 4). Internet shopping cards target teens. *The Gazette* (Montreal). Entertainment Express, p. C10.

Quality selection criteria for subject gateways. (1999). *European Union Desire Project* [Online]. Available: http://sosig.ac.uk/desire/qindex.html [2000, November 7].

Rainie, L., Kalehoff, M., & Hess, D. (2002, Sept. 15). College students and the web. *Pew Internet and American Life Project* [Online]. Available: http://www.pewInternet.org/ reports/toc.asp?Report=73 [2003, October 27].

Ready or not, the electronic mall is coming. (1994, November 14). *Business Week,* i3398, 84.

Reed, J. (1999). Blue web'n. In A. Wells, S. Calcari, & T. Koplow (Eds.), *The amazing Internet challenge: How leading projects use library skills to organize the web* (pp. 36–52). Chicago: American Library Association.

Reengineering through information technology. (1993, September) [Online]. Available: http://govinfo.library.unt.edu/npr/library/reports/it09.html [2003, 13 May].

Resource Discovery Network. (2003). *History* [Online]. Available: http:// www.rdn.ac.uk/about/history/ [2003, June 6].

Reuters. (2000, August 17). Study focuses on kids and advertising. *The New York Times* [Online]. Available: http://www.nytimes.com/2000/08/17/technology/17kid-ads.html [2000, November 1].

Reuters. (2003, December 24). Yahoo! to buy software maker. *Los Angeles Times,* Section 3, p. 2.

Reynolds, E., & Plucker, J. (1999, May). Panning for gold (creatively) on the new frontier: Locating and evaluating educational resources on the Internet. *NASSP Bulletin, 83*(607), 8–15.

Richmond, B. (1998, May/June). CCCCCCC.CCC (Ten Cs) for evaluating internet resources. *Emergency Librarian, 25*(5), 20–21.

Riley, R. W. (1996). Executive summary, getting America's students ready for the 21st century: Meeting the technology literacy challenge. *U.S. Department of Education* [Online]. Available: http://www.ed.gov/Technology/Pln/ NatTechPlan/exec-sum.html [1999, July 21].

Robins, K., & Webster, F. (1999). *Times of technoculture: From the information society to the virtual life*. London: Routledge.

Rosenfeld, L. B. (1994, Winter). Guides, clearinghouses, and value-added repackaging: Some thoughts on how librarians can improve the Internet. *References Service Review, 22*(4), 11–16.

Saettler, P. (1990). *The evolution of American educational technology*. Englewood, CO: Libraries Unlimited.

Safford, B. (1996, November). The problem with the Internet is NOT the information highway. *School Library Media Activities Monthly, 13*(3), 42–43.

Salpeter, J. (2003). Web literacy and critical thinking: A teacher's tool kit. *Technology & Learning, 23*(8), 22–34.

Samoriski, J. (2000, Winter). Private spaces and public interests: Internet navigation, commercialism and the fleecing of democracy. *Communication Law and Policy, 5*(1), 93–114.

Sanger, E. (1990, May 7). Teaching the TV generation: Cable companies look at the school set and see a new generation of potential subscribers. *Newsday*, p. 4.

Sarnoff, D. (1936). In C. S. Marsh (Ed.), *Educational broadcasting 1936: Proceedings of the first national conference on educational broadcasting* (pp. 147–155). Chicago: University of Chicago Press.

Schechter, D. (1999). *The more you watch the less you know: New wars/(sub)merged hopes/media adventures*. New York: Seven Stories Press.

Schlender, B. (1996, July 8). A conversation with the Lords of Wintel. *Fortune, 134*(1), 46.

Scholz-Crane, A. (1998, Fall/Winter). Evaluating the future: A preliminary study of the process of how undergraduate students evaluate web sources. *Reference Services Review, 26*(3/4), 53–60.

Schwartz, J. (2000, November 2). Offer of free computers for schools is withdrawn. *New York Times*. [Online]. Available: http://www.nytimes/2000/11/02/technology/02COMP.html. [2000, November 2].

The Scout Portal Toolkit. (2003). *Internet Scout Project* [Online]. Available: http://scout.wisc.edu/research/SPT/ [2003, November 20].

Siegal, N. (2000, June 7). Sell the scene, not just the shirt. *New York Times*. Available: http://www.nytimes.com/library/tech/yr/mo/biztech/technology/07sieg.html [2000, June 7].

Silverstein, K. (1998). *Washington on $10 million a day: How lobbyists plunder the nation*. Monroe, ME: Common Courage Press.

Smith, A. G. (1997). Testing the surf: Criteria for evaluating Internet information resources. *The Public-Access Computer Systems Review, 8*(3) [Online]. Available: http://info.lib.uh.edu/pr/v8/n3/smit8n3.html [2000, November 7].

Smulyan, S. (1994). *Selling radio: The commercialization of American broadcasting, 1920–1934*. Washington, DC: Smithsonian Institution Press.

Solock, J., & Wells, A. T. (1999). Scout report signpost (signpost). In A. Wells, S. Calcari, & T. Koplow (Eds.), *The amazing Internet challenge: How leading projects use library skills to organize the web* (pp. 203–222). Chicago: American Library Association.

Spring, J. (1992). *Images of American life: A history of ideological management in schools, movies, radio, and television.* New York: State University of New York Press.

Spring, J. (1997). *The American school, 1642–1996.* New York: McGraw-Hill.

Stakes are raised by Net advertising. (1999, August 4). *The Financial Times,* Inside Track, p. 8.

Studebaker, J. W. (1936). United States Commissioner of Education. In C. S. Marsh (Ed.), *Educational broadcasting 1936: Proceedings of the first national conference on educational broadcasting* (pp. 22–29). Chicago: University of Chicago Press.

Sussman, G. (1997). *Communication, technology, and politics in the information age.* Thousand Oaks, CA: Sage.

Technology for America's economic growth. (1993). *Clinton technology policy initiative* [Online]. Available: http://simr02.si.ehu.es/DOC5/nearnet.gnn.com/mag/10_93/articles/clinton/clinton.tech.html [2002, April 5].

Tedeschi, B. (2000, July 3). Giving consumers access to personal data. *New York Times* [Online]. Available: http://www.nytimes.com/library/tech/00/07/ cyber/commerce/03ecommerce.html [2000, July 3].

Thoburn, P. (2000, July 3). Canada leads world in wired schools. *Strategy* (The Canadian Marketing Report), 23 [Online]. Available: http://www.strategymag.com/articles/magazine/20000703/youth-wired.html [2000, August 14].

Walters, C. (1999). The future for children and the Internet. In C. M. Macklin & L. Carlson (Eds.), *Advertising to children: Concepts and controversies* (pp. 281–284). Thousand Oaks, CA: Sage.

Waters, R. (2003, March 12). Search industry scours scrap heap for bargains. *The Financial Times,* p. 30.

Watson, J. S. (2001, October). Students and the world wide web. *Teacher-Librarian, 29*(1), 15–19.

Websites warned to comply with children's online privacy law. (2000, July 17). *Federal Trade Commission release* [Online]. Available: http://www.ftc.gov/opa/2000/07/coppacompli.htm [2002, January 7].

Welcome. (1997). *AT&T* [Online]. Available: http://www.att.com/communityguide/welcome.html [1997, October 19].

Yahoo! (2002, November 13). Yahooligans! names the hottest toys based on kid picks. Press release. *Yahoo!* [Online]. Available: http://docs.yahoo.com/docs /pr/release1022/html [2003, June 21].

Young, J. R. (2002, February 22). Ever so slowly, colleges start to count work with technology in tenure decisions. *Chronicle of Higher Education,* pp. A25–26.

Zoll, M. H. (2000, April 5). Psychologists challenge ethics of marketing to children. *Mediachannel.org.* [Online]. Available: http://www.mediachannel.org/orginals/kidsell.shtmllroot=528 [2000, April 18].

Zollo, P. (1995). *Wise up to teens: Insights into marketing and advertising to teenagers.* Ithaca, NY: New Strategist Publications.

Zook, G. F., President of the American Council on Education. (1936). In C. S. Marsh (Ed.), *Educational broadcasting 1936: Proceedings of the first national conference on educational broadcasting* (pp. 3–7). Chicago: University of Chicago Press.

Index